Cuban Bread Crumbs

Cuban Bread Crumbs

Jack Espinosa

To order additional copies of this book, contact:
Xlibris Corporation
1-888-795-4274
www.Xlibris.com
Orders@Xlibris.com
45009

Contents

BOOK I

Virginia

BOOK II

El Puente

BOOK III

Somos Como Somos

Dedication

This is for Cerelina Alfonso Espinosa, a love at first sight that became perpetual, who never stopped believing in me, gave me two sons and two grandchildren, none of whom has ever given me a single moment of shame . . . and who somehow managed to survive over half a century of . . . . ME.

Acknowledgements

Cuban Bread Crumbs is a work of love. It is not the accomplishment of a single person, but rather the result of hundreds of donors who provided me with unforgettable experiences over a lifetime. The stories written in this collection required much help from others, too many to mention, without whom I would have aborted this project in its early stages.

With no knowledge about the myriad processes of managing the publication of a book, I sallied forth with limited writing skills and much insecurity. It took an army of friends and family members to arm me with the audacity to continue. I especially owe heartfelt thanks to my editor, Bill Duryea, who not only offered to take on the job, but insisted on doing it. Bill is one of the many reporters who covered the "crime beat" in Hillsborough County for the St. *Petersburg Times* when I was the Information Director at the Hillsborough Sheriff's Office. A consummate professional journalist, honest and ethical, he is among the very finest I have ever dealt with. When he told me he was excited and genuinely enjoyed reading my stuff, I knew I was going through with it. Now an editor with the St. *Petersburg Times*, Bill dedicated his valuable time off from his very busy job to help me with this work. Another "angel" in my life.

Special thanks to: Ferdie Pacheco, my super prolific friend, world renowned author, physician and artist, for the painting used in this publication, and, more important, for the inspiration his life has been to me; Patrick Manteiga and father Roland, editors of *La Gaceta* for their support and help throughout the years; Albert Gonzalez, educator and artist, for the sketch he painted for this book; John W. Parker Jr., photographer/artist responsible for all reprints and original photos, including the cover; and my fellow "roaches," Sicilians, Spaniards, Cubans and Anglo "Crackers" who made my life worth living over again.

Jack Espinosa
Tampa, Florida, 2007

Editor's Note

I did not edit this book. Jack Espinosa does not need an editor. I rode shotgun on a publishing odyssey. I laughed far too much for it to be considered work. This is the way it has been since that moment 17 years ago when I first encountered Jack—entertaining the "media corpse," as he called us—at some now long forgotten crime scene. I was a very nervous reporter, but Jack made me laugh when all I could think about was that I would be fired if I didn't get this story in on deadline. Poking fun at me, everyone around me and anything else he could think of, Jack communicated a very important message: Relax. This is nothing, he was saying. Even as he was delivering the most dreadful news in his unfailingly professional manner, Jack's irrepressible storytelling reminded us of what really matters. Stories matter, because good stories, funny and poignant stories, bind people together. Stories make communities.

Reading this book is like listening to Jack and listening to Jack is how I learned nearly everything worth knowing about Tampa. If you happened to grow up in Tampa, perhaps during that dynamic moment in mid-20th century when Ybor City was really humming, then you'll much find much to cherish in these chapters. But this is more than a nostalgic memoir. If there is an underlying theme through these stories it is how a scrappy generation of kids from immigrant families bridged two cultures and in doing so transformed America. As with all of Jack's stories Cuban Bread Crumbs is told with such warmth and humor you feel a strange envy for not having lived it with him. That's what good stories can do.

Bill Duryea
Tampa, October 2007

Introduction

Like the Canterbury Tales, which I learned to enjoy in Middle English thanks to the brilliant Dr. Howard G. Baker at the University of Tampa, these short stories are windows into a time past worthy of remembering. I am no Geoffrey Chaucer, but like the old master storyteller, I've tried in my own limited way to reflect the lives and times of my generation born in America of Spanish, Cuban, Italian/Sicilian immigrants who settled in Ybor City, West Tampa and Palmetto Beach around the turn of the 20th century. Each tale stands alone. No attempt was made at any particular chronology, although stories are arranged to reflect a logical sequence of time from approximately 1900 to 1950—more or less the time it took us to get "Americanized."

This is not a historical work, although there is a thin thread of history going through each tale. It is more about the people of the time than of the time itself. For a grand work on the history of this era look to the recently published Ybor City: The Making of a Landmark Town by scholar and dear friend, Frank Trebin Lastra.

Authenticity of each story is completely dependent on my own remembrance as told to me by original sources, or, as in most cases, as I myself experienced them. Liberties were taken on exact times, places, and some names due most to loss of memory over the years. Several names were invented to fill in the blanks or to protect the guilty, but most are correct. None of these omissions change the veracity of the stories.

This work attempts to portray the inventive characteristics of the human spirit when people find themselves having to survive isolation in a foreign environment. The struggle to become "American" belongs almost exclusively to first generation offspring of immigrants. The unique culture that evolved in Tampa from that struggle is what these stories are about. My generation served as the bridge between the country of our parents and the nation that became ours. As the old mixed with the new, beautiful threads were woven into the magnificent fabric that is America.

This small offering attempts to shed some light into that recent past with the hope that it will inform, entertain, amuse and foster appreciation for our differences . . . and to better illustrate why we are as we are, "*porque somos como somos.*"

Book I

Virginia

Virginia Acosta, age 17, Tampa, 1911

Chapter One

In the Beginning

"Is Quien tied up?" asked Maria Acosta as she knocked on the door of the Morejon family. Holding Maria's hand tightly was her ten year old sister Virginia. "Quien" had been barking and growling incessantly from the time the girls approached the fragile, unpainted frame house. They had walked well over two miles to spend some time with Fulgencio and Dora Morejon's two pretty daughters.

Quien was a large mixed-breed dog with a dangerous disposition. He was kept tied to a mango tree in the back yard after having attacked and seriously injured several people in the community. His vicious reputation was widely known. So feared was the hound that people went a block around the house to avoid his intimidating howl. Twice he managed to escape his enclosure causing loud panic in the neighborhood.

Puerto Camarioca is on the northern coast of Cuba about 40 miles east of Havana. Populated mostly by *guajiro* farm hands and fishermen, some doubling as dock workers, the town is not even shown in detailed National Geographic maps. It was on that remote spec of the world that Virginia Acosta was born in a thatched-roof *bojio* with no flooring but the hard earth. Daughter of Spanish and Irish immigrants, Carlos Acosta and Caridad Salazar Fowler, she was the youngest of five children, three boys and two girls.

Morejon's daughters were delighted to see the Acostas. Visits were treasured in a world where people were isolated from company by distance and lack of transportation. Most walked. Only a privileged few had horses, carriages or even donkeys. A motor car was from another world. Nights came fast after long working days, so poor people ate their dinner and followed the chickens to slumber. Visits were a highlight usually reserved for Sundays.

Dora hurried out of the kitchen nervously wiping hands on her apron as she happily announced the arrival of the visitors. *"Maria y Virginia! Que bueno, llegaron a buena hora."* ("Maria and Virigina! How wonderful, you've arrived at a good time.") Any visit at whatever time was always just in time to eat something—an old custom among Cuban families. Being poor meant nothing. Whatever there was in the kitchen, if only a cup of black coffee and bread. The evening supper was often sacrificed to the visitor. Taught early to politely refuse such kindness, the Acostas were too embarrassed to take anything.

The four girls sat in the front room—giggled and laughed and talked about school, games and all those beautiful things that young girls talk about. Being the baby, Virginia had little to say as the teenagers carried on.

With one powerful final shake Quien broke loose from the harness and quietly headed full speed toward the intruders of his domain. Laughter turned to screams as Maria dashed out the front door with Quien in pursuit. The dog ignored all but the fleeing victim. The chase was short business. With one terrible lunge, Maria was knocked down onto the dusty road. She put her hands up to protect her pretty face as the beast tore into her white neck. All near the scene ran for cover. Some climbed trees. Virginia, still in the house hiding behind a chair with the other girls, quickly abandoned her protection when she saw her besieged sister, now face down as the dog bit her back and neck. At full speed she streaked toward the fry, jumped on Quien's back, grabbed him by the ears and pulled back with all her strength. Managing a strangle hold around the dog's neck, she wrapped her thin legs around his body and rode the animal as she bit the back of his head. Sufficient to give her sister, now bleeding profusely from deep wounds about her entire body, time to crawl away from the ordeal. Finally, the dog's owner got to the tragedy and pulled the animal away from Virginia's clutching arms and legs.

Both girls were treated for wounds at the scene as best as could be expected and taken by wagon to a clinic some miles away. Virginia was badly bitten and scratched on her arms and legs but luckily survived the inevitable infections that followed. With no antibiotics and little else than alcohol and peroxide available to treat wounds of such magnitude, Maria met a slow, painful death that mercifully ended her suffering.

Had Quien chosen to attack the baby instead of Maria, I would not be alive to tell the story. The heroine of Camarioca, praised by one and all for her fierce courage in defending her sister against a frightening animal became my mother some years later in a magic land far away called Ybor City.

Little is known about my mother's early years in Camarioca. She related few stories about those times in her life. I am not sure if she was trying to forget or that she was too young to remember much. Information was scant but enough to give me some "flavor" of that side of the family tree. Her stories were mostly pleasant or funny with the exception of her sister's terrible death. She spoke so much about her mother that I feel as though I know her. Caridad refused to have any photos taken because she didn't want her children to be forever grieving her death. What a tragedy for me who can only imagine an auburn haired grandmother with aqua blue eyes and a face like an angel as described by my mother. Mama idolized her, especially after losing her at such a young age. Carlos, my grandfather, had one photo taken for which I am ever grateful.

My grandfather on my mother's side, Carlos Acosta

My son, Christopher, looks so much like him. Both my mother's parents died within a year of each other and shortly after Maria's tragic death, leaving Virginia to face those difficult teen years with no parents. Her three brothers took over her tutelage and fiercely protected her. Perhaps it was this strict vigilance during her most vulnerable years that accounts for her staunch skepticism about all things. It was hard to put anything over on her. Sharp, intelligent and wary she developed a toughness that served her (and me) well throughout life. Although strict in protecting the family "honor" my uncles were all very funny guys as must have been my mother's uncle Federico of whom she spoke often.

Federico was self-taught but showed a keen talent with words. His poetry was a bit raunchy but still worthy of praise. An example, according to my mother and verified by my uncles, was a poem that he wrote on the wall of an outhouse he had built on some rocks that hung above the seashore. A fisherman by trade, Federico spent much time just offshore in a rowboat he had made. With no facilities in the small inlet where he spread his net, he used the shed to meet his needs as he cleaned his catch on top of the rock. Convenient indeed because there was a natural hole in the rock formation that jagged out over the oncoming waves which crashed against the rocks and pushed refreshing sea water up the opening. Astutely, Federico put the four walls around the hole and topped it with an inclining thatched roof. An opening on the leeward side served as entrance covered with a rice sack curtain. An old bottomless chair placed directly over the hole in the rock served quite adequately as the toilet. Ingenious! Robinson Crusoe could not have done better.

A single poem adorned the wall facing the chair. It's the only one my mother remembered and passed it on to me for posterity. It read:

> *El que venga aqui a cagar;*
> *Que se fige con disimulo;*
> *Como les baten el culo;*
> *Las frescas brisas del mar.*

Perhaps someone more closely possessed by the Muse can render a better poetic translation to English, but this is the best I can do:

> He who comes here to shit;
> should note unimpressed;
> how his ass is caressed;
> By the fresh breezes of sea.

Never saw Federico, but I feel I know him. My uncles were equally humorous each in his own way. Was there any question that Virginia could be anything, but never dull!

Her fame as a comedienne was legendary in Ybor City where she and her three brothers had come to work in cigar factories. It didn't take her long to become an accomplished "*rolera*" (roller) and to gain popularity more for her hilarious antics than for her remarkable courage and toughness.

I was a reckless eight-year old playing a couple of houses from my home. As clueless kids do, I jumped into a clump of high weeds where a hidden broken bottle bottom was sticking straight up. I landed face down and got a deep stab wound on my left thigh. Blood gushed out of the deep cut and ran down my leg soaking my shoe with bright, crimson gore. I dashed home screaming so loud that I even alarmed our neighbor, old lady Librada who was stone deaf. My father was sitting on the swing in our large front porch and first to see my left leg now drenched in blood from thigh to tip toe. Yee-Ya, Yee-Ya (short for Virginia) he shouted before falling into a stupor and nearly passing out. Fortunately for me, my mother was home for lunch still wearing her cigar roller apron. Enter steel lady into the panic. She grabbed the source of the bleeding with her left hand pulling the sides of the open wound together then wrapped her free right arm around my wrist, lifted my little body and sitting me on the porch railing. She then hugged my neck, put her lips on my forehead and softly whispered, "esto no es nada, Cuquito. No llores." (This is nothing, Coquito. Don't cry.) Rocked me ever slightly back and forth while still clutching tenaciously to the wound enough now to have stopped the heavy flow. She ordered Salvador (my father) to run inside and get my brother Hector who was in the back yard unaware of the accident. Papa managed to recover somewhat from his shock and dashed to get my brother. Salvador had committed diarrhea along the way as Hector came to the scene. Mama told my wide-eyed brother to bring his bicycle. She sat me on the handle bar and with his help rolled me to the Gonzalez Clinic (El Buen Publico) four long city blocks away. Mama never let go of the bone-deep wound which was almost sealed by the time we got to the clinic.

Stitched and bandaged, I was returned via Hector's bicycle which he used to deliver morning newspapers. When we got home to 16th Street my mother kissed my brow, brushed away dirt, perspiration and a few remaining tears. She then returned to work at the factory on Michigan Avenue (now Columbus Drive) and 16th Street. The red-brick building with the tower clock is still there. She changed her bloody apron and finished her quota (*tarea*) of 500 cigars (cinco ruedas) not one whimper, not one tear—she never lost her composure through it all. Her stout-hearted courage and loving touch melted away all my anxiety and fear. Florence Nightingale could not have been better.

Virginia Acosta Espinosa, age 36

Chapter Two

El Machetazo

Grandmother Carmen was native of Cadiz, Spain. "La Curra," as people from there are called (Curro for male) had left Spain around the turn of the 19th century with her young son, Salvador and her second husband, Jose Rosas. Reasons for their leaving Spain were never made very clear to me but rumor had it that Salvador had gotten into some serious trouble when at an annual religious festival he had put feces on the feet of a statue. What made it even worse was that it was the patron saint of the village which parishioners devoutly stood in long lines to kiss. That was probably the last straw in a long train of irreverent manifestations he leveled at authority. My grandmother took him out of Spain under the pretense that he was a bit mentally deranged and that he was having difficulty with his eyes. The move was first to Havana, Cuba where presumably one of the world's best eye surgeons (Castroviejo) practiced. Not clear how they did it, but from Havana they came to Tampa and remained here for the rest of their lives. Lucky me because it was here that my father, divorced from his first wife, married my mother also a divorcee. He had a son, Antonio, from his first marriage and my mother had two sons, Lionel and Hector Carreno. Both were in their late 30's when I was born.

Mama came to Tampa with her three brothers, Joaquin, Iginio and Eufemio when she was in her early teens. She learned to roll cigars and became an accomplished "rolera" earning a meager income depending on how many cigars she and her "bonchero" could make in one day. Output depended on the skill and speed of two people, one "bunching" the various grades of tobacco and putting the required blend together (tripa) for the particular cigar they were making and the other rolling the "tripa" (guts) or the inner cigar with the outer leaf "capa" that gave it the proper shape and held the smoker together. Five hundred cigars was considered a good daily output. Most could not reach that quota (tarea) of five "ruedas" (rounds). Each round being 100 cigars. It was hard, exasperating, tedious labor in dusty environs with no air conditioning or adequate heat. A short break for lunch made an eight or nine hour day very long. It was after that long day that mama went home to cook dinner and tend to her bedridden mother-in-law.

In 1929 my grandmother was struck down by a terrible stroke that totally paralyzed the right side of her body. My mother took care of the old lady as if she were her own daughter. There was no such thing as a nursing home among Cubans, Spaniards or Sicilians. Old folks were an essential and in some cases an indispensable part of the tribe for good or for ill, in good times and bad. When the old folks left the house for good, it was on a one-way trip to the cemetery. Rushing home after work, preparing dinner for seven or eight people and tending to the multiple needs of a paraplegic took a Herculean effort. After cleaning bed pans, changing linen, bathing and feeding my stricken grandmother, mama was able to spend some time with me as we sang, danced and did jokes for abuelita's enjoyment. My grandfather, Jose would baby sit with the old lady whenever mama and I went out which was very rare. Time spent with mama was usually limited to weekends. Before I started school, Jose and maybe some of the old guys that rented rooms in our house sort of watched out for me. I pretty much had the two-story house to myself and a small back yard with chickens, ducks, and a goat. The street and anything beyond my next door neighbor's house was off limits until I started school at age six.

Carmen is the only grandmother (abuela) I know. So proud was that woman that she refused to be taken out of her room because she didn't want anybody to see her condition. When mama made the bed she would put her in a home-made wheel chair next to the bed. Carmen refused even to be rolled out to the porch! At one point she went on a hunger strike refusing to eat or drink anything but a little water. She did not want to be a burden to others. My mother told me that when she became pregnant with me, the old lady decided to live after going over one month without any nourishment. Unbelievable, but true! What's even more incredible is that when she finally decided to eat, she wanted whatever had been cooked for dinner that day. My father contacted Dr. Portocarrero of El Buen Publico Clinic who advised that she take only light broths and then soft food over a period of days until her stomach readjusted to a regular diet. Consuming solid food after so many weeks of fasting would surely kill her. Her Andalusian stubbornness vetoed such treatment. She ordered a plate of black beans, rice and pork left over from dinner. Family gathered and after much deliberation decided to let my father decide. "If she's going to die, let no one say she died of starvation—she died full!" He filled a plate with all she ordered and placed it before her. She gummed the food (no teeth) swallowed chunks and lived to change my diapers using her only good hand and gums! She died when I was eleven.

Crime in Ybor City was uncommon. Once in a while you'd hear of a burglary and now and then a Mafia shooting made big headlines. Funny how syndicate killings were taken for granted. It was accepted as something that happens only to those people involved in illegal business. My family never feared such attacks. It was between "them." I am sure that there were a lot more crimes committed that were not reported such as spouse and child abuse. Drug crimes were unheard of although alcohol use was quite prevalent. Police presents was extremely rare. Only place I saw cops was on Seventh Avenue our main commercial street. My mother spoke sparingly about some "marijuaneros," guys who smoked pot. People walked everywhere at all hours with no fear of being attacked or robbed. Contrary to some who say that they slept all night with open doors during those days, the people I knew locked theirs. You knew you had grown up when Papa allowed you to have "el llavin," the key to the house after much lecturing about handling this responsibility.

One very cold winter night we were huddled around our two-burner heater in my grandmother's room. The rest of the house was like an ice box so when it was time to go to bed we would put on our coats and go to our rooms where a cold bed awaited under an avalanche of "frasadas" (blankets) and a heavy "quito" (quilt). Cold was conquered until time to get up in the morning. After I had done a few songs and some funny stories (imitating some acts I had seen at the Cuban Club Theater) mama and I sat at a small table by the heater to play cards. After a couple of games of "la brisca," my mother stopped, put her index finger to her lips and listened. "*Calla*," (quiet) she whispered. The old lady had fallen asleep as a great chill came over me. A subtle thumping sound came from the back door to the kitchen. Someone had unlatched the screen door to the back porch and was now trying to get into the house. Our back door was shorter than the frame by over a foot leaving ample open space at the top. The door had no lock. It was secured with a two-by-four wooden latch that crossed the door and fit into metal braces on each side. Standing on a chair from the back porch, the burglar had stuck his arm through the opening at the top attempting to dislodge the latch. I was the only "man" in the house. All others were at the Centro Espanol playing dominoes. All we had to defend ourselves was a paraplegic old woman, a five year old baby and Virginia Acosta Espinosa—poor burglar. We couldn't tell what was actually happening, only the faint sound of wood rubbing against metal. Virginia again put her finger to her lips, took me by the hand and walked slowly in the dark toward the noise. I was so petrified with fear that I couldn't even whimper, totally suspended in space yet I remember every single step. She took a machete off the wall that my father had hanging in the kitchen next to the kerosene stove. With me holding her left hand she stealthily approached the long right arm of the intruder now more visible as he was still trying to lift the latch. She had to get close because the light switch to the kitchen was next to the door. With the speed of lightning she let go of my hand, switched on the light and began to whack the man's arm just above the elbow twice before he could get his arm out of the opening. It was a very white arm in a white, long-sleeved shirt that was pulled to safety amidst horrifying screams. The burglar flew out the unlatched screen door. The force of his departure was such that the hinges, screen and frame of the back door were found strewn all over the back yard. He jumped over the back fence knocking over the trash can that we had sitting on the platform atop the fence for the garbage collector. All we heard were screams and the noises of someone letting nothing get in his way to get out of where he was. Mama showed no fear as she swung into action and no sign of mercy once she began to swing the blade. If the machete had not been so dull we would have had a bloody arm as evidence. The bloody trail left from kitchen to back fence was proof enough. Trembling enough to induce a bowel movement, I stood pale and motionless as I puckered up trying to avoid the inevitable tears at the sight and sound of it all. Mama hugged me tightly, "No es nada, mi amor, no es nada" (It's nothing my love, it's nothing!)

After making sure she was rid of all danger, we went back to my grandmother's room and continued the card game after we both had a shot of jerez wine. When grandma awoke she asked what had gone on. Mama told her that it must have been a cat, "No need to upset the old lady," she whispered as she winked.

To my knowledge, my mother had fear of nothing—except a frog. Yes, a *frog*! I've never been able to figure out why a woman who fought a vicious killer dog, faced adversity with calm courage and attacked a burglar with a machete would pass out at the sight of a little green tree frog. I saw her cry twice in all my years and very briefly at that. Nineteen forty two and two of my brothers were somewhere in the middle of a war. Mama and I were celebrating the coming of the new year hoping against hope to see the end of that terrible conflict. She was sporting a pointed red hat and blowing a little horn as she paraded around the tiny upstairs bedroom in our apartment at the Ponce de Leon Housing Project (a giant step up from our former abode, at least we had cold and hot running water.) At midnight the familiar "Auld Lang Syne" was played as mama increased the volume on our little radio. All was joy and happiness as the air raid siren on top of the housing project went off in harmony with the horns of City Hall and the shipyard on McKay Bay (also known as La Draga.) After the traditional musical greeting and this being a time of war, Guy Lombardo's band struck up the Star-Spangled Banner. It has never sounded better. Still clowning for my sake, she stood up straight like a soldier at attention and saluted smartly as our national anthem filled our hearts. I quickly stood up and returned the salute. That's when it happened. Virginia broke down! I was stunned. A moment in my life unforgettable, burned into my memory forever. For the first time I realized that the "Iron Lady" was just as vulnerable as we mortals.

Recovering almost immediately, she continued to march around the room blowing her horn in rhythm with the music that followed. It would be some time later that I saw a second tear from those big brown eyes. It was when Franklin Roosevelt died.

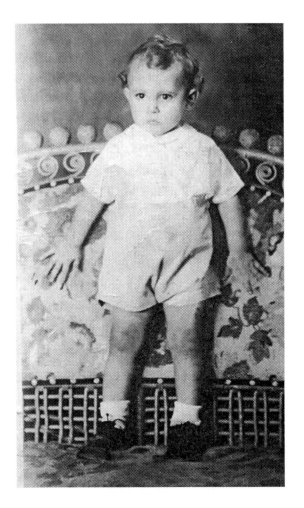

Twenty-two months old, Joaquin Eugenio Espinosa
(Couquito)

Chapter Three

Yankee Doodle Mama

July Fourth was the best day of the year. It was the one time I got to go to the beach. Especially meaningful because my birthday fell on the fifth and birthdays were not celebrated (in fact they were ignored) in my home. No candles, no cake—none of that nonsense. My Iberian folk made no fuss about getting a year older. I learned about birthday parties later when I became more "Americanized." I have never had a birthday party. Some note was given to the day of your patron saint but not much-ado about that either.

Arriving at 1611 11th Avenue just 15 hours after American Independence Day was fortunate indeed because cigar factories were closed on the 4th so I celebrated my birthday a day earlier when many of us isolated souls got a chance to go to that enchanted land of salt, surf and snow white sand—CLEARWATER BEACH! Whoever coined it "Sparkling Clearwater" sure knew what he was doing. Papa, who was never too fond of water, had better things to do like playing dominoes, smoking cigars and spitting on the floor at the Centro Espanol, so mama took on the ordeal. "Mama Virginia (as her grandchildren call her) would book a round trip on a flatbed Caltagirone Warehouse truck for that long sojourn to the Gulf of Mexico via Safety Harbor and Dunedin. There was no Courtney Campbell Causeway then.

The trucks were a beautiful dark green though they had little surface to paint. No windows or windshield with a very scant roof over the cab, the vehicle was mostly open to the elements and a mere link above its horse driven ancestor. A long vertical column with a large steering wheel stuck up from the wooden cab floor. Tires were solid rubber. A chain wrapped around a small wheel on a shaft near the engine extended and wrapped around a larger wheel in back to propel the hauler. Motor was started by setting the ignition on the steering column while a crank sticking out from the front of the engine was turned by some hearty individual who chanced a broken limb from a kickback. Sitting on the floor of that flat bed required passengers with courage and stamina. At 40 miles an hour rolling on solid rubber tires above those old roads made the tortuous ride particularly tough for the older people. For us kids it was heaven, especially when false teeth rattle and more than once lost when a large pothole was hit. I saw a pair of dentures fly out of Dionicio's (the butcher) mouth hitting and sticking to a woman's hair net. We laughed our asses off.

Trip there was always fun. Coming back was another story. Packed with tired people and three washtubs with little ice for what was left of the watermelons and the Nehi sodas (all part of the deal) the portable fences inserted into the slots on the sides kept us from falling off, especially the men who took shots of whiskey now and then chased with beer. If it rained (and it usually did) it was greeted as a benediction refreshing our overheated bodies. The lightning, however, was a bit harrowing at times.

Two days before the trip my anticipation became unbearable. Going anywhere outside my eight-block boundaries or beyond the streetcar terminals was wonderful. A trip to the beach was the ultimate pleasure. No one in my family had a car until I was ten when my oldest brother bought a Dodge. I got little of that because he got married and moved away. Neither of my parents ever dreamed of driving a car. Streetcars, buses (later) and walking was the way to go anywhere.

Night before the trip was sleepless so when the alarm went off I was starring at the clock as it reached five a.m. Mama made two pea omelettes and nestled them between two pieces of Cuban bread. It was all you could do to keep from eating the sandwiches immediately. Breakfast was Ybor City tradition—buttered Cuban bread and Cuban coffee with evaporated milk. Dunking was (and still is) proper etiquette among the more civilized natives of Ybor and our colony West Tampa. Sandwiches were wrapped in old Gaceta newspaper and placed in brown grocery bags. With my brother Hector's black woolen bathing suit rolled into a towel under my arm we walked four and one half bocks to the Caltagirone Warehouse on Tenth avenue and 20th Street where we loaded up to depart at eight a.m. We were lucky to get to the Clearwater Pier by ten thirty at which time I would go behind a bush and put on my brother's bathing suit. It was at least two sizes bigger than my skinny waist. No matter, it was beach time and I could have cared less that even the black leather belt holding up the suit was overlapping a half length.

After a blinding sprint through sandspurs and silver sand I dove into the Gulf of Mexico and remained in it till it was time to leave around five p.m. I had around six hours of sea, sun and sand delight. It was the big pay off for all my yearning and anticipation.

My mother stood at water's edge the whole time like a hen watching her biddy, making sure I was safe. One day a year for a scant six hours of beach frolic was so precious that I would not eat (not even watermelon) until the time to return. It was considered suicide to return to the water after eating until at least three hours had passed. No matter how hungry I was or how much mama insisted. I would not eat. For me it was poor economics to trade three hours of beach time a year for a pea sandwich! I ate it later no matter how soggy. The hen made sure there was a good-sized piece of watermelon left. She has always taken care of me. Once out of the water for good, my skinny, burnt, wrinkled, ugly little body was in desperate need of replenishment. Cold watermelon was ambrosia of the gods. I devoured all mama put in front of me right down my parched esophagus. I'd been in the water so long that my lips were a pale purple. In spite of July heat, I trembled, chilled to the bone marrow and if we got rain on the way back, my feverish little body shook and my teeth rattled.

I knew that Independence Day was important but not sure why. Ironic that the son of Spanish immigrants would wind up teaching United States History in public school. I spent whatever time necessary to implant that second paragraph of the Declaration of Independence into the minds of every single student. It is the rock upon which this democratic republic is built. Still, every time I explained the meaning and importance of that document—I always thought of the beach.

When I reached my 12th July, things were a bit different. The war made money a little more available so now we could afford to travel by bus. This trip we took a bus to downtown Tampa, where we boarded a Greyhound Bus to Clearwater city and then yet another to the beach. Although air conditioning was not yet in buses, it beat the hell out of those old trucks. It was difficult to travel anywhere during those war years. Two of my brothers were in the Army and we were reluctant to go anywhere. It was considered detrimental to the war effort to waste fuel for any except the most essential trips. Travel priority was to be given to servicemen. We felt a little guilty, but rationalized that one little trip to Clearwater wouldn't hurt the war effort. "Is this trip really necessary?" read signs at all bus and train stations with Uncle Sam pointing a long finger at you.

It was on that excursion in 1943 that I learned a great lesson about America, one that I will cherish forever.

When we boarded the bus in Clearwater to take us on the last leg to the beach, my mother took the only empty seat available. It was next to a black woman on her way to work. She never noticed (or didn't care to) that there were several white people standing. The bus driver abruptly stopped the bus and slowly worked his way through the crowd. Tall and in a blue uniform, he approached the auburn haired woman sitting next to the "colored" lady. In a very deep, official tone, apparently trying to impress the standing whites, he told her that she had to move because colored were to occupy seats from rear forward and white from front to rear. Mama had a pretty good idea of what he was saying, but she played her "I no speak the English" card and asked me in Spanish, "*Que dice?*" I was beyond petrified with fear. Anyone in a uniform was scary even a bus driver. I could hardly speak. Feebly I told my mother in Spanish what the order was. By the look on her face I could tell that she was pissed off and ready to take him on. "*Dirle al hijo de puta este que lo prieto de esta mujer no se me va a pegar, y que ella es tres veces major que el. Yo no me muevo. Que vall a freir esparagos!*" (Tell this son of a bitch that this woman's color will not rub off on me and that she is three times a better person than he is. I am not moving. He can go fry asparagus.") I felt sure we were going to jail and worse yet—no beach! The black woman attempted to get up but my mother held her by the arm. They looked at each other and without a word decided to stick together. With my voice trembling and teary eyed, I informed the man that she was too old and didn't understand the rules or the language. I didn't have the cojones to translate the message, especially about frying asparagus. The driver pushed his blue hat back, shrugged his shoulders and said, "These goddamned Cubans are all niggers anyway," walked back to the front and drove off. The two ladies looked at each other and smiled ever so slightly. My day was saved. No jail!

Virginia Acosta Espinosa never read the Declaration of Independence, not even the sentence that says "all men are created equal . . . ," but her inner sense of justice and her courage made her an American patriot of the first line most appropriately on that hot Fourth of July 1943.

Chapter Four

The Great Reginsberg Stickup

There was no way I could go to a party or any other gathering of older folks from Ybor City or West Tampa without someone approaching me laughing and saying something like, "are you Virginia's son? Let me tell you what your mother did . . ." Her fame as a humorist permeated cigar factories on both sides of the Hillsborough River during her years then grew to legendary status after she died and went to that other funny place.

I remember as a little boy how often she embarrassed me with her audacity. Some of the stuff she did was not funny at the time. It was only after I finally grew up that I realized just how hilarious her stunts were. Like the time we had gone out for a walk to get some sherbert at Los Helados De Ybor. Famous for sandwiches *mixto* (real name of the popular Cuban sandwich) and multi-flavored sherbets, Los Helados was located on the corner of 14th Street (now Avenida Republica de Cuba) and 8th Avenue, several blocks from our house and two blocks south of the Circulo Cubano (Cuban Club.) As we walked by the Circulo we heard music coming from the theater on the second floor. It was the overture to a *bufos* play and variety show played by a two-piece band (piano and timbales, a small kettle drum.) My mother loved *bufos* and much to my delight, decided to use our sherbet money to see the show. Problem was that there was only enough in the treasury for one adult ticket. "Oh well," I surmised, "I guess we can't go." Mama, however showed no sign of retreating to sherbert. Up the long stairs we went to the small ticket booth where she bought one adult ticket with her last coins. I had thoughts of her leaving me outside the theater while she enjoyed the show. "Naw, mama wouldn't do that." Then I began to worry about what trick she had up her sleeve. She then took me by the hand, told me to keep my mouth shut and walked straight through the entrance. The ticket-taker tore her ticket in half, gave her the stub and asked, "*y el nino?*" (and the boy?) to which she responded very quickly, "*bien, gracias*" (fine, thank you) and

Believe it! That's me at age 4. No wonder women loved me.

whizzed on through. Rufina, the ticket-taker who knew her well, split a gut laughing and repeated the story for years.

Then there was another incident told many times over among factory workers about my mother's most audacious antic. I learned of it from Tomasa Alfonso, better known by her nickname (as was the case of so many in Ybor and West Tampa) "La China." China (pronounced Cheena) was mother to Frank and Jerry Alfonso, among my very closest friends. We like to say, "like family" about hundreds of close friends collected over the years in our small communities. Being that so many of us have made Tampa our life-long home, we virtually have thousands of close acquaintances. Hillsborough County and Tampa in particular have a large native population. We just can't live anywhere else, which explains why we are so friendly and why we seem a bit "clannish" to outsiders. That is changing as oldsters pass on and newcomers arrive by the thousands.

China was my mother's best friend. An angel of a woman and very beautiful, China was a very reserved, quiet person who pampered her two boys like fighting cocks. Kind and giving, non-intrusive with a delightful naivete. I have such fond memories of her. China laughed at everything my mother said or did. With that kind of audience, my mother had a ball doing a variety of special shenanigans for her pal's delight. With her natural angelic innocence, La China was the perfect counter to my Loony Tune mother. It was like Groucho Marx and Margaret Dumont.

The big clock on the tower of the Reginsberg cigar factory (El Reloj) showed both hands pointing to 12. A hot, sunny summer day and workers were having lunch. Many stayed in their places but some went to the Mercedes Restaurant (first Spanish/Cuban cafeteria) one block away. Others just sat outside on the concrete and rod iron fence at the entrance of the property that occupied an entire city block on Columbus Drive and 16th Street.

Tomasa and Virginia chose to sit along the fence just north of the entrance to the factory. They munched on sandwiches downed with cold drinks bought at El Reloj Grocery located across the street. The little store was owned by a lovable, smallish, bald headed Spaniard, Pancho (Francisco) Garcia and his wife, Inez. Hard to believe that our food was purchased at small family owned stores no that long ago. Pancho kept track of what we got during the week and paid our debt on Friday or Saturday—a thing of the past.

The ladies were about finished with their lunch when the Brinks armored truck rolled up to the entrance to deliver the payroll. Operators were a driver and a guard in back. No windows at the rear of the vehicle just a few slits in the walls of the truck for the guard to peep out in search of possible robbers.

One of the men was a friend of our family and especially close to my next door neighbor and godfather, Eugenio Fernandez. Albertico (little Albert) Rey was a short, pleasant fellow with a rotund waist line probably in his late 40's at the time. Albertico (little Albert) was unusual in that he had jobs that were rare among us. For one thing, he did not work in a cigar factory. He had been a semi-tractor driver at one time and drove a car-carrying truck right up to my godfather's house on 11th Avenue. You would have thought there was a three alarm fire the way folks came from all the neighborhood to gawk at this incredible thing. Imagine that! A truck carrying four brand new Ford sedans. Wow! Of course, Albertico's pay was a good bit above cigar workers, so these factors made him somewhat of a celebrity among us. This stature gave him a look of importance and a certain smugness especially when he spoke of his many exploits on the road. When he later took the job as a Brinks' armored car driver and guard, his pomposity rose by several lengths.

When the truck was parked, the driver walked around back looking vigilantly in all directions. With left hand on his pistol he knocked on the back door for Albertico to open. Both in uniform, complete with visor caps and side arms, Rey climbed out of the vehicle with a short-barreled shot gun. The other guard walked up the long stairway and entered the building. Quickly observing the ladies sitting on the fence, he lit up like an incandescent bulb. He really put on a show for them. Looking from side to side and giving passersby a suspicious, menacing look. Short, bald, fat and blimpy, he made a very comic "macho man."

"Watch this," my mother told China as she stealthily walked around the truck when Albertico was looking the other way putting on his act for some other ladies. She stood on the side of the truck opposite the factory entrance where she could not be seen by the other guard. When the driver yelled down from the top of the stairs that the office was open and ready to receive the payroll, Rey leaned into the back of the vehicle to fetch it. Bent over with his large rear sticking out, he stretched to grab the sack. That's when Virginia stuck her index finder into his ribs and yelled, "STICK 'EM UP!" Shotgun and coveted payroll sack dropped and Albertico went flying into the truck.

Much to his credit, ever the trooper, Rey quickly recovered from the shock. Recognizing the culprit, he hugged her and managed a nervous laugh as the ladies roared and applauded the show. La China got sick laughing and could not finish her lunch. Even Albertico's partner was laughing. How does anybody get away with such things? My mother must have an angel taking care of her.

Chapter Five

False Attack

Virginia was beloved by all who knew her. Everybody likes to laugh, even Pietro Longo who spoke a very limited Spanish. My mother was very adept at picking up foreign languages and had learned enough of the Sicilian dialect prevalent among immigrants from that island to carry on regular conversations. That was bit unusual among residents of our colony. Being the smallest of the minorities, Sicilians more likely learned Spanish. Both Cubans and Spaniards spoke Castilian, making Spanish the dominate language among the residents of Ybor and West Tampa.

For a couple of years Longo was her bunch-maker and he was glad of it. She was not only a very fast cigar roller, but much fun to be around. Since it was piece work, a good team could make more money than the slow pokes. He did his best to keep her happy to insure that she remained with him and not move to another factory or change partners. Longo was very frugal to say the least and worked at times through lunch to keep up with speedy Virginia. If one of the team got sick the other would lose the day's work. In those days it was a very serious matter.

Virginia was not her usual, jolly self. Somber and quiet, she moaned once in a while as she held her hand up to the side of her face. "*Que te pasa, Virginia?*" (What's wrong?) asked the lady across her bench. "It's a terrible tooth ache I have that's kept me up all night! It's been like this for two weeks, but today the pain is unbearable," she replied. After a while she moans again a bit louder from the excruciating pain. The left side of her face even looked swollen at the cheek. Longo was showing great concern as the situation got worse with each passing moment. Losing the entire day was a disaster of the first magnitude. Perspiring profusely after several more of mama's groans, Pietro offered to get some aspirin. She accepted the offer with a very feeble, painstaking, "O.k. Longo, here's some money," He refused to take anything, "*De ninguna manera,*" (no way) he said. "I just can't stand to see you suffer," as

Ready to fight for the Republic of Ybor City in full uniform, Capt. Couqui Espinosa, age four. Photo taken at Vanart Studios on Franklin Street in downtown Tampa, 1935.

he ran down the aisle to the first floor and then out the front door to Papito's drug store, La Economica, across the street where he bought two aspirin tablets. He returned like a paramedic handling an emergency. Completely out of breath, after taking his large body down and up those steps at full speed, Longo delivered the relief. Someone else had already gotten a glass of water. Virginia, looking pale and sickly, slowly downed the tablets leaning her face away from the side of the painful tooth as she swallowed. "Relax and give it time to work," advised Carmita another "roller" across the line. Virginia heroically kept rolling cigars in spite of her ailment. To suffer pain and discomfort for the good cause is among the greatest of virtues. Longo kept on making bunches as fast as he could, holding his breath in the vile hope that she would at least last till noon. A long silence came over the entire "galera" (gallery of workers in rows.)

"*Hay, que dolor!*" (Oh, what a pain!) The loud lament broke silence and returned despair. All hope that Virginia would stay ended abruptly. "Virginia, you've got to pull that tooth out," Carmita advised. "Absolutely right, Carmita that's what I must do," answered Virginia as she reached into her mouth, pulled out her dentures and threw them on the table.

Modern-day cigar roller making cigars just like my mother did 70 years ago.

Chapter Six

Pepe's Wake

I was on my way home in my immaculate 1947 Chevrolet after a long day as a substitute carrier for the U.S. Post Office. It was around 5:30 on a hot August day in the early 50's when I spot my mother waiting for the bus on the corner of 7th Avenue ant 15th Street. The usual thunderstorm had been brewing for sometime and some of those large summer raindrops were beginning to splatter against the hot street pavement and hood of my car.

Tapping the horn twice I hollered, "*vamos vieja*" (come on old lady) as I beckoned her to get in the car. She runs to the curb and jumps into the front passenger seat. "How wonderful," she said, "and just in time," as she pointed to the approaching deluge. "I'm not going home, I have to go to Pepe's wake over at Lord and Fernandez funeral home. Just drop me off there." The dark heavens opened up and down came rain so heavy that I had to pull over and park.

"You've got to come in with me, Cookie (my nickname) even if just for a moment to pay your respects to the family," she said. "Mama, I don't even know the deceased," I replied, trying to get out of it. I'll introduce you to him," she quipped with a very straight face. Right away I forgot how tired I was. This was going to be fun.

The old cigar maker (*bonchero*) had been on a two-week vacation at Clearwater Beach with his son and family when he suffered a sudden heart attack and died. All his fellow workers from the "*chinchal*" (a small individual proprietorship with a few workers) were among the mourners. Many "retired" cigar makers worked in these small operations to supplement their Social Security. Some were located in individual homes. Conditions in the chanchales were less hectic. Workers produced what they could or what they chose. The boss was usually the owner who often worked right along with the others. The line between worker and management was practically non-existent. Under such intimate conditions, oldsters enjoyed their closing years and took care of each other—just like family. It was a beautiful thing to see. If someone did not show up to work his fellow workers would find out why, since many lived alone and prone to all the ills of aging. My mother was employed at the chinchal and very close to all the cast of characters there who had been friends for many years.

Going to the beach was still a big deal even in the fifties but like most of the new generation, Pepe's son, Armando, had benefited from the upswing in the economy due to the Second World War. Having served in the Army, he had taken advantage of the G.I. Bill and gotten a good education and career, but two weeks at the beach was still an unusual treat.

Pepe's death was unexpected even at the age of 84. He had shown no symptoms of heart disease, worked hard every day and lived a life relatively free of illness. Maybe the fresh salt air and sunshine or being away from the domino game at the Centro Asturiano for more than a week did him in.

As we lined up to view the body, Pepe's roller, Carmela, wept quietly. She had been half the team with the old man for some years. A bit younger than her partner, Carmela stood out from the crowd. Doggedly refusing to appear her age, she was conspicuous wherever she went. For one thing, she weighed in at around 220 pounds and only five feet, five inches tall. She carried two enormous breasts that marched on before her by a quarter of an hour, dyed her hair an alarming mix of orange and brown, painted her large lips a dark red all the way up to her nose and powdered her face heavily to contrast with rosy rouged cheeks. Her broad shoulders tapered down to a well strapped waist then exploded out to an immense derriere. From behind, her ass looked like a gigantic valentine. Upon this body she wore a flower-patterned dress that she must have put on with a spray gun. A surprise meeting with Carmela in a dark alley would stampede the Virgin Mary! Amazingly, her gaudy appearance magically disappeared when she spoke to you. She had a pleasant, engaging personality. Everybody loved Carmela who took Pepe's death as if she had lost a loving father.

"*Hay Couqui, no somos nada.*" (Oh, Cookie, we are nothing") she cried loudly as she hugged my neck. "We are nothing" is a common adage among Spanish-speaking people at funerals and wakes. Carmela held my mother's hand as the line moved slowly to give Pepe a last look. As we approached the casket, Carmela moaned as the tears flowed freely down her colorful cheeks. "Look at Pepe," whimpered Carmela. "How well he looks, as though he were sleeping." "Why shouldn't he look well?" retorted my mother, "He spent two weeks at the beach!"

Sadness turned to mirth as it got around the funeral home. Carmela laughed and cried, laughed and cried, laughed and cried . . . till she peed in her large pants. Even the widow laughed. And when the story got around the cigar factories the next day all of Ybor City and West Tampa laughed.

Chapter Seven

Tumble on 21st Street

With a bag of groceries upon each arm, Virginia, now in her 70's, stepped off the bus at the corner of 21st Avenue and 16th Street near Cuscaden Park and just one block from our home. The bus was packed with mostly cigar makers going home. As she planted her left foot on the last step, she tripped and flew head first out the door. Bus driver and a couple of men sitting up front jumped out to help. They helped her to her feet and asked her if she was hurt. Just a little scrape on the knee. She was fine. They helped her pick up the groceries. Nobody is laughing yet but with the realization that she was unharmed, a relaxing sigh of relief comes over the commuters. Insidious half smiles appear here and there among the faces of the witnesses apparently waiting for the bus to move on so they can laugh. After all this is Ybor City. Mama is aware of the general mood knowing full well that if there are no serious injuries, an old lady flying out of a bus with two bags of groceries is funny as hell! Everything back in the bags, except a few broken eggs, she thanked the driver and the other helpers assuring them that she was fine. Then seizing the moment, she turned back to the passengers who were holding back their laughter and says, "*Esto es una democracia, cada uno se apea de la guagua como le sale del culo.*" ("This is a democracy, each person gets off the bus however it comes out of their ass.") In Spanish "comes out of their ass" is vernacular meaning "however it damned well pleases you." In all my years in show business as a comic, I've "stopped the show" many times, but I've never stopped a bus. The little old lady with the auburn hair now more gray than auburn, slowly walked away with the naïve, Jack Benny look that she was famous for. The bus stayed parked for several minutes as the bus driver busted a gut laughing together with the throng in the passenger seats and standing.

Her statement was not only funny but very profound. It is one of the most descriptive ways to define our freedoms in America. Many of the old timers that lived in our community and now their offspring often use the adage when their actions or opinions are questioned. I use it often as do my family. I cleaned it up a bit and had mama's statement inscribed on parchment, framed and hung in my classroom when I taught United States History and later in my office.

"THIS IS AMERICA. HERE EACH PERSON GETS OFF THE BUS AS THEY PLEASE."

Virginia Acosta Espinosa

Chapter Eight

Exit La Cucaracha

Weekend call outs were common for me as Information Director (Public Information Officer) for the Hillsborough County Sheriff's Office. It was my last and most rewarding of many careers. As spokesman for the agency I handled most of the news media's requests for information. If you had told me back in the 1950's when I was working as master of ceremonies and top banana at strip joints that I was going to end my career in a law enforcement agency, I would have thought you were crazy! More than that, I wound up working for the beat cop that patrolled Franklin Street where the joint was located! Walter Heinrich was the officer and he was elected Sheriff years later. A dear friend and consummate professional, I always joked about how I worked for a cop that looks like Dick Tracy (and he does.) For a former stand-up comic, I sure took my job seriously and although it was no requirement for me to be on call 24 hours a day, seven days a week, it was my own policy to be on scene as much as possible. I wanted to make sure I knew what was going on and not "behind the story" where reporters knew more than I did. Walter Heinrich and later Cal Henderson, two of the best lawmen in the county were easy to work for—they let me work as many hours as I wanted. Forty eight or even 72 hours straight on some of our most newsworthy cases was not uncommon. I would often chide that the best thing for law enforcement was a good standup comic.

Murder at a pizza restaurant in Brandon on a Saturday morning was big enough news for me to respond. Weekend reporters are not the regulars that cover crime stories during normal working hours. That makes it all the more important for me to handle sensitive information that if misunderstood or released too soon could foul up an investigation.

The body of a male employee was found early on a cool Saturday morning Nov. 4, 1989. Call from dispatcher got me out of bed around 0400 hours.

Sleep has never been indispensable to me. It's too much like being dead. I've never wanted to miss anything.

My mother, now 95, had been living with me and my wife, Sally for almost ten years. Cerelina Alfonso Espinosa whom I call "Mother Cerelina" makes Mother Teresa look like a Nazi. She was the first to insist that my mother come live with us when she became too sick (and forgetful) to take care of herself. Stricken with Alzheimer's disease, she knew we were related, but not who we were. Never cross or difficult, mama was still a pleasure to be around. If there is any justice on earth, my mother was abundantly repaid for what she did for my father's mother. My blessed wife and I took care of her all the way to the end. If she had her senses, Virginia would have never agreed to live with anyone. She knew not who we were nor where she was. Her case was unusual in that she actually realized that she could not remember and would often fake recalling events and people. I like to say that mama remembers that she forgot. She still did her funny stuff albeit repetitious. She laughed heartily at all my jokes and antics which I could repeat to infinity and still get a laugh. Trips to the hospital became more frequent as the end came near. We were ready for the worse when she would fall into deep comas. My wife woke me up one night when mama was in a coma. We listened to her recite a poem over twenty minutes long apparently written by a young man who rode a white horse. It must have been someone she was very fond of early in her life. I wish I had recorded it. She never missed a single word. In her revelry, she repeated it. I had never heard that beautiful offering before.

Showered quickly, put on my suit and tie and headed to crime scene at the pizza parlor in Brandon. As customary, I called all news organizations via my car phone on the way. The victim had been shot to death with a small caliber handgun. Fortunately, it was no "who dunnit," the crime was solved quicker than usual. Sheriff's detectives found evidence tying a co-worker to the shooting and by 0900 hours the suspect was charged and arrested. Usual briefing followed and all were packing cameras ready to take the story to air. A few questions remained unanswered as is the case in most investigations and reporters would be contacted throughout the day with various details as they became available. Even a simple case like this one would drag on for the rest of the weekend.

In the middle of the news briefing, the Communications Center (dispatcher) had radioed a message to me and when a deputy handed me a note, "call your wife immediately, urgent," I knew it had to be something bad. My wife had never called me at work. I got back to her as soon as possible after having "fed the animals."

Mama was seriously ill and taken to the hospital. By the tone of Sally's voice, I knew it was curtain time. When I got to the hospital she met me at the door of the room. "She's gone," Sally said tearfully, it's all over for her now." Strange how we are all aware of the inevitability of death and yet no matter how expected, it is always a shock. No one spoke for about five minutes. We just held on to each other. Death is so unacceptable.

One of the nurses who had known me for most of my life came up to me, cupped her hands around mine tightly and said, "Jack, I'm so sorry," as tears filled her eyes. She knew how much that little old lady meant to me. A long silence enveloped us all.

"Maybe this is not the right time to tell you, but Jack," she continued, smiling as she sniffled. "Her last words were not spoken, they were sung. Your mother was singing La *Cucaracha* as she faded away."

She did it to me again! What an exit!!! In her last moments she let all know that dying (*No es nada, mi amor*) is no big deal. She looked at the boney face of the Reaper and then danced into the next phase of all this mystery we call life singing about a roach!

Our tears blended beautifully with our laughter. She must have planned it that way. Joan of Arc was an amateur—a piker. Virginia had more *cojones* than a Roman Legion. She sent death packing with its tail between its legs.

Even in death, it was vintage Virginia Acosta Espinosa, the toughest, wisest, fairest, funniest, most loving, most unforgettable and most influential person in my life.

Some people should live forever.

Book II

El Puente

Grandmother Carmen Rosas Espinosa Benitez Munoz y
Ballesteros (La Curra), age 40.

Chapter One

Katuka's Christmas

Noche Buena (Christmas Eve) at 1611 11ᵗʰ Avenue was the best night of the year. In fact it was tops for any Spanish, Cuban or Sicilian resident of Ybor City or our beloved colony, West Tampa. Being recent immigrants, Christmas in 1937 was celebrated in our homes pretty much the way it was in the mother country. Santa Claus during my early years (1931-39) sort of crept up on me and eventually replaced "Los Reyes" (kings bearing gifts for the Christ child.) There was not too much fantasy for me as a child. Life for those Spaniards had been very difficult and they had little time for play. They did, however, have some fanciful stories to liven things up a bit, much like the Irish, very tough people but still blessed with a bit of the "blarney."

All of my relatives on papa's (Salvador's) side were Andalusian (southern Spain) famous for producing show people, artists, Jerez wine, flamenco dancers, bullfighters and most of all, bull-shitters. Also called "Curros," my ancestors were famous for guitar playing, drinking and story-telling, never letting facts interfere with a good yarn and a bit apt to exaggerate. When a "*Curro*" tells you that he was attacked by a pack of wolves, feel free to reduce the pack to perhaps a couple of dogs, probably Chihuahuas. When I asked my father if there was a Santa Claus, he put his hand on my four year old shoulder and very solemnly said, "No." Yet, he had me convinced that the moss on the trees were growing remnants of the beards of Spanish conquistadores torn off their faces as they tramped through the woods long ago looking for a fountain that produced life-giving energy and youth.

Noche Buena (literally Good Night) certainly lived up to its name as rich, poor and poorer stretched what resources they had to make the night before Christmas special in every way. In one great show of benevolence, Papa would walk into the kitchen and proudly reveal the contents of a brown paper bag he carried, throwing three or four cans of peaches on the table. He did this every year with an air of pomp and ceremony. It made me very happy. So much so that I would keep the labels showing those beautiful yellow/pink peaches and paste them on pieces of cardboard. Our home was very lucky. We had less means than some and more than many, many others. An advantage in my house was that my grandmother brought over enough money to buy two houses in Ybor City. The house where I was born was a two story frame building with seven bedrooms and two baths. Extra rooms were rented to fellow Spanish immigrants who had no family here and who seldom paid rent. Things were tough and Papa didn't have the heart to throw them out, so they became part of the family contributing food and helping with expenses. A large family with three or four tenants provided enough money to pay for a substantial "*cena*" on Noche Buena and a gift for the baby—me.

Early morning December 24, the aroma of a "*pernil*" (fresh leg of pork) roasting in sour orange and garlic marinade thickened the air in our small community and filled the populace with a joy impossible to explain. It was as though all the world was my family. Everybody knew who he was and where he belonged. Really, I have never needed anything more than what I had then—health, family, friends, and the feeling of belonging. What beautiful memories I have of those happy days when we lived sans television, sans central heat or air conditioning, sans automobiles, sans refrigerators or electric stoves . . . and for me, sans worries.

A 25 pound leg of pork, having received the Cuban benediction (three days marinating in sour orange juice and garlic) was removed from the ice box, nestled in a large iron pot and placed atop two flaming burners on a kerosene stove. My mother had started cooking at 6 a.m. following procedures dictated by the loving and beautiful tyrant of the household—"*abuelita*" Carmen Rosas, Espinosa, Benitez, Munoz y Ballesteros, my grandmother, "*La Curra.*"

From her bed, this mother of my father controlled all matters relating to the dinner. She was partially paralyzed from a stroke that completely took all feeling from her right side. Once a stunning beauty, her face was now disfigured, her right hand withdrawn into the shape of a claw and her right leg severely twisted, rendering her totally immobile. For fourteen years she imprisoned herself in her bedroom, too proud to let anyone except family and closest friends look upon her. Not one day started for me without my first going to her bedside and giving her my "*buenos dias, abuelita,*" a kiss and a hug. This ritual was mandatory before I even washed my face or brushed my teeth. Mama made sure of that.

On Noche Buena she allowed herself to leave her self-imposed cell to attend the "*cena*" in the dining room. My mother would dress her up in a white gown and my cantankerous grandfather, Jose, was allowed to place the old lady in a homemade wheelchair made out of a regular chair nailed onto a wooden square of two-by-fours. Wheels were four well-greased, smooth rolling Union skates left over from a Christmas past and bolted onto the wooden frame. Upon this thrown she was wheeled into the dining room where we all awaited her at the table that had been set in accordance with her wishes. Her annual pilgrimage was very special.

Mama spent all day in the kitchen. With only three burners the pig took priority as garbanzo soup, black beans and white rice awaited their fire. The salad of lettuce, tomatoes and "*berro*" (watercress) was last.

An interesting admixture, my family, three step-brothers, two Carrenos from my mother's first marriage and one Espinosa from my father's first. I was the baby. My mom was born in Camarioca, Cuba of Spanish Asturian and Irish parents while Papa's were from Cadiz, Spain. No one spoke about my Papa's blood father. To this day I don't even know his first name. Mama whispered to me once that he reputedly drank "mucho vino," played the guitar and cavorted with "bad women." Papa's step-father, Jose Rosas, Galician (Galicia Spain) by birth was the only grandfather I knew. Both of my mother's parents had died before I was born. She was brought to Tampa as a teenager by her three brothers Joaquin (my namesake) Iginio and Eufemio, my most beloved uncles. So many children without fathers and here I had five, not counting Manuel and Bachiller, two of those tenants that never paid the rent. Manuel would take me on long walks down to Sixth Avenue to see the trains until he laughingly told my mother one day that he had to help me (during an emergency) remove my short pants to do "*la caquita*" on the railroad bed. Mama turned pale. "Suppose a train comes by and runs over the baby!" Everybody laughed except my mom who sternly referred to Manuel as "*un idiota*." Bachiller, the other tenant, took cussing to a very high level—a poetic art form. Cussing in Spanish (in those days done almost exclusively by men) is in my estimation the most ferocious and nasty concocted by man. Abuelo Jose was no slouch, in fact his poetic genius approached Bachiller's. Jose's very large, round, hard head engendered few beneficial ideas and the few he did mange were rigidly fixed. There was no utterance in his vocabulary that remotely approached the English word "compromise." His stubbornness (and my father's) was responsible for our poverty. Convinced that the Crash of 1929 was not for real, they refused to stand in line at the Broadway Bank and consequently lost my grandmother's small fortune ($8,000.) The blunder was undoubtedly a chief contributor to the stroke that crippled her.

With all those people and two police dogs (Jackie and Nellie) living under one roof; rabbits, chickens, two turkeys and a guinea hen in a very small back yard, my toddler years were full of activity. To make our lives even more interesting, my oldest brother's future father-in-law, a West Tampan of Cuban parentage, "El Guajiro," liked me so much that he gave me a little nanny goat picked out of a large herd he kept on Grace Street. She was my first very own pet. I nursed and loved that animal like only a five year old can. My mother named her "Katuka," after a feisty comedian who starred on a Cuban radio show broadcast nightly from Havana. By Christmas Katuka had grown to a substantial size and got along fine with the menagerie. There was some adjustment necessary, but in time the two dogs ignored the intruder as long as she stayed outside or in the back bedroom that had been converted from a screened porch. Mama had allowed me the luxury of putting my little bed there so I could sleep with Katuka, whom I loved more than Timmy loved Lassie.

The house was full of people by six on that memorable Noche Buena. Among the few outside invitees was my father's best friend whose name I never knew because everyone called him by a nickname to which he nonchalantly responded. This phenomenon was very prevalent in Ybor City and West Tampa. "El Visco" (The Cross-eyed) was the ugliest man I have ever seen. His eyes were acutely crossed, mouth twisted to his right side, and (as if to insure that none would ignore his calamitous countenance) he defiantly adorned all this with a monstrous Mongolian mustache that marched downward around his mouth from his nostrils to his lower jaw. In addition, a bicycle accident had rendered him lame so that his left leg would drag up to meet his right as he walked. A bachelor, of course, he was what Jimmy Durante would have called, "a catastroscope." When he walked together with my father, whose toes pointed away from each other (like Charlie Chaplin's) it was indeed a site to behold!

Family and friends gathered at the old house by six. The men had already hit the bottle of Corby's with some regularity. Talk was getting louder and laughter even more so. Joy filled every corner as all moved downhill toward the dining area to await "La Curra's" grand entrance. "El Visco" was sitting on a stool next to the unlatched screen door that opened into the back porch when Katuka entered the room uninvited from the backyard. I can still see the look of alarm on his face as he tried to grab the nanny goat. Jackie and

Nellie began to bark boisterously as they ran forward to protect their turf. The ruckus that ensued was like a scene from a Marx Brother's movie. Barking, howling, growling, bleating, yelling, screaming accompanied the tumbling bodies of humans trying to grab and separate the animals. The goat tapped around the linoleum-covered floor as the dogs pursued under and over the table and chairs. At one point, Katuka stopped, turned, and assuming a defensive posture, lowered her head and charged into the dogs and the crowd. Visco was down, Papa was down, Mama was at ready with a wooden spoon, my brothers all struggling to grab the snarling dogs.

"The Cornered Goat and the Flying Abuela" by Ferdie Pacheco, a special gift from a dear friend.

Into all this comes Jose pushing the wooden wheelchair with grandma upon it like a Napoleonic cavalry officer. In the confusion, Jose forgets his first responsibility and lets go of the wheelchair. From the door entering the dining room, the floor declined acutely toward the rear of the house. The angle became even more pronounced going into the back porch. With wheels so well greased, here comes the old lady barreling downhill completely unnoticed in the continuing melee. By the time the chariot from hell hit the entrance to the back porch it looked like the 12th Avenue streetcar hauling ass! Mama yelled out, "*la vieja, la vieja,*" ("the old lady, the old lady") to no avail. By the time her dilemma got our attention she had already plowed into the back wall of the house, cussing at Jose. My grandfather ran to free the old lady who was now pinned against the wall. By inches she had missed flying out the door into the yard. Nervously, he asked, "*Te lastimastes, vieja?*" (are you hurt, old lady?) Abuelita Carmen Rosas, Espinosa, Benitez, Munoz y Ballesteros—La Curra, picks up the small metal bell she carried to call for service and hits Jose on his large, round bald head and said, "*Tu madre, viejo cabron!*" (your mama, you old goat!)

Chapter Two

Palanca

Vicente Martinez Ybor Elementary School was a tough place in 1938. I had just transferred over from catholic school located half block from my birthplace, a two story frame house, 1611-11th Avenue in old Ybor City.

Tuition at Our Lady of Perpetual Help was .25 cents per week and my mother (Virginia) afraid of my having to walk alone five city blocks to "the free school" on Michigan Avenue (Columbus Drive) and 15th Street, sacrificed the quarter so I could be closer to home. My father (Salvador) was not too supportive of the idea not so much for the high cost, but because his experiences in Spain with the church were not exactly pleasant ones. Papa was pretty close to anarchist. He loved America because, "there is less government here than any place else," he would often say. With some grumbling, he acquiesced to mama's protective instincts. She always got her way anyhow—diplomatically or otherwise.

After one year, both my parents decided that I was not learning much. How they came to that conclusion is puzzling because neither one of them could speak English nor got involved in school activity. There was no PTA, no welcome parents day, no teacher parent conferences. If you didn't behave you'd get thrown out and if you didn't pass you repeated the grade. Attitude toward education was, like most everything else for Papa, very, very simple.

"If you don't pass, you go to work and if you don't respect the teacher, '*te parto un tarro*' (I'll break one of your horns.) That's Castilian for hitting you on the head. In any case, they decided to send me to free school.

The straw that broke mama's back was when she mistakenly sent me to school on a Friday with a chorizo sandwich. I would have gotten away with it but the smell betrayed me. I have never trusted a chorizo again! When I removed the oily, brown Cuban bread wrapper, all the kids knew what I had.

Bzoulfohs. MY FATHER
SALVADOR ESPINOSA

Papa Salvador took this photo in Havana on one of his many excursions there. He sent me this photo/post card with the message: "Para mi querido Couqui con todo mi alma, querido hijo. Tu padre, S. Espinosa." (For my beloved Couqui with all my soul, dear son. Your father, S. Espinosa.)

First they snickered, then they started laughing as the Cuban bread crumbs inevitably fell on the clean long table in the lunchroom. Wearing short pants to school was bad enough—now this—a chorizo eater! Not only a greasy, oozing chorizo eater, but a chorizo eater on a Friday—mortal sin!

Sister Teresa swooped down on me like the Avenging Angel, took the dripping devil's food, wrapped it back up and threw it in the trash all in one great motion. Together with the chorizo went a slice of guava paste pressed between two matching pieces of yellow cheese hidden in the back of the greasy bag—dessert. The nun then hit me eight times on my little knuckles with a 12 inch ruler which she carried unseen wherever she went. The kids laughed their asses off. I was so ashamed, so horribly humiliated that I began to make funny faces, playing to the crowd as though I didn't mind it all. The Angel apparently had no sense of humor and hit me four times on the head with the magic ruler. It stopped the funny stuff, but I didn't cry. Not in front of the girls.

Being six years old is a wonderful thing. By the time I got home, I had almost forgotten my ordeal and when mama asked me her daily question, "?comistes hijo?" (did you eat all your lunch?) I hesitated. I was afraid to tell her what had happened. When I finally did, her eyes squinted, her lips tightened and then asked, "did they give you anything to eat?" I was horrified that she would run to the nunnery and make a spectacle of us all, but I had to tell her the truth. I even defended the nun's action.

"Mama," I pleaded, "it's a sin to eat meat on Friday's."

I never told her about the knuckle shots.

"They should have given you something to eat," she said grimly.

Eating during those years was very, very, very important. That's why old immigrants from that time put so much emphasis on food. Fat was attractive. It was a sign of prosperity. A measure of prestige. The practice persists to this day, even with the new generation. Wonder why we have fat kids? No one can get near my house today at any hour and not hear my wife repeat our mother's or grandmother's greeting—"you're just in time to eat something!" And if you refuse, they'll shove it down your throat.

Mama never made a scene when I was left "lunchless" but the following September I enrolled at the free school. My very Andalusian father put me back in the first grade, having decided that I had not learned anything that whole first year! I was one hell of a whiz in class (I could speak some English) but I remained one year behind other kids my age through the 12th grade. A formidable first year in private school was not enough for Papa Salvador. I heard him proudly tell his friends from Spain (who rented rooms in my house but never paid) that now I was going to learn "la democracia."

"Baby class" at Our Lady of Perpetual Help School, 1936. That's me sitting on the ground, fourth from the left. Photo courtesy of Ladie Alvarez, lifelong friend who is standing top row, second from left

Most V.M. Ybor kids were as poor as I while a lot of others were much poorer. I got a whiff of democracy my very first day. On my way home as I innocently skipped along (like Pinocchio going to school) I was attacked by about ten guys. The leader, "Chato," older than the rest, was very muscular with a rather pronounced lower jaw and a receding forehead. He grabbed me by the neck and threw me into a human ring his followers had made. They then proceeded to beat the hell out of me. I can still feel the grit of the sand in my mouth when I was knocked down and kicked. They did it in front of some of the girls too.

Quite a difference from my former, docile education at Our Lady of Perpetual Help and I quickly learned a precious lesson, one of those enlightenment's in life that has "perpetual" value. Security, I have since surmised, is always at the expense of freedom and vise versa. Catholic school offered total clarity and security. Everyone knew exactly what NOT to do, although not always knowing what TO do. Authority was total and exacting. All things went along with medieval rigidity. Lines were straight and true, your every move was under surveillance and any deviance, however small, brought instant reprisal. The omnipresence of authoritarian rule permeated all thought and deed insuring a total sense of security not only in school but in the community. A priest once paddled a boy and made him kneel on dry corn kernels for hours when he learned that the rascal had taken some tangerines from a neighbor's tree on the way home from a movie on a Saturday morning. So, the long arm of the theocratic dictatorship reached out to wherever you were, exacting order and security. When we did our little misdeeds, someone would always say, "don't let the priest find out." That was next to impossible because the whole adult neighborhood was in on it.

Within that enclosure (maybe six blocks of Ybor City) I was safe! No fights, no bullies, no danger . . . and no freedom. I never worried about anyone kicking my ass except the priest, a nun or my parents—total security was mine.

The "Free School," as the name we gave public school implies, was indeed free. I remember how delighted I was when I found out that every hour we all got up and moved to another class with a different teacher. Freedom of movement, a breath of fresh air, talking, pushing, shoving, cursing and other assorted freedoms flourished. When you asked to go to "the basement," where the toilets and urinals were, you went by yourself, enjoying the freedom to wander around a bit. But, of course, as I soon learned you were wandering bait for a sucker punch ambush from behind a locker or crevice administered by Chato or one of his disciples.

Sporting a slight shiner and a broken lip from my first encounter with freedom, I noticed that members of Chato's following were making faces at me and giving me a variety of unsavory signals with their fingers. Chato kept clinching his dirty fists and pointing them at me, indicating that I was going to get a lot more of what I had received on my inaugural "independence" day.

It was frightening. Especially when he would bring his fists (one at a time) up to his gritting green teeth, pumping his arms back and forth. The other lap dogs began obediently doing the same as their leader. Between classes, as I "freely" moved about, I got shoved a bit and told of the impending "*golpes*" (beating) that awaited me after school. The bad guys did not know about my speed, however and they spent the next two months chasing me home from school. It was like the coyote and the road runner every day. I spent a goodly time each day figuring out different ways of getting out of the school building without getting caught. Once I was out, nobody could catch the flash. My terrified existence was a secret. I wouldn't tell anyone for fear that my mother would find out and—well, you know what. I even managed to disguise my black eye and the painful gash I had on the inside of my lower lip.

Somehow my older brother, Hector (by ten years) found out what was going on. I begged him not to tell mama. He wouldn't do that. He was not exactly fond of her going out with me in hand and kicking the shit out of those bullies. How embarrassing! She might even do it in front of the girls!

Hector Carreno, dearest big brother—my mother's son from a previous marriage. He was always there when I needed him.

Hector gave me the solution. I later learned what it is called. It is called "*palanca*" (leverage.) The wheel is not man's greatest invention—it's "PALANCA." It has served me well over these long years.

Here was the plan:

A—hide three feet long, two-by-four piece of lumber behind bush next to the alley behind the National Garage (corner 11th Avenue and 16th Street)

B—when turning into alley (with gang coming up behind) pick up "*la leña*" (the lumber)

C—holding the lumber by the end (to give proper leverage, (*palanca*) administer "*leñazo*" (stroke) to the first son-of-a-bitch that comes 'round the corner;

D—continue to swing "*la leña*" hitting as many as possible.

Brother Hector would be standing by in case the plan didn't work. It worked. After a guy named Pino (first one around the corner) regained consciousness and the "*chichon*" on his forehead subsided a bit, the gang quickly and unanimously agreed that I was nuts and left me alone forever.

It was the way of survival at the free school where professional boxers attended classes with children in order to learn English. A physical education teacher was knocked out by a 16 year old boxer in a fight that broke out in the hall during school hours!

Looking back at my terrifying ordeal, only the very first of many more to come, I realize the importance of those experiences. I'm glad I went to the free school where I learned yet another invaluable lesson. Palanca, not the wheel, is man's most important invention and anything free is very expensive.

Rare automobile in Ybor City in the late 1920s. Proudly standing with a Tampa cigar in his mouth is Angelo Arbesi (El Gago), carpenter deluxe and close friend. In driver's seat is Eugenio Fernandez, later to become my godfather. Sitting in the back are Papa Salvador and my oldest brother, Antonio (Nico) Espinosa. Photo taken in front of our house at 1611 11th Ave.

Chapter Three

Alfredito

That first generation born of the group of Spanish, Sicilian, and Cuban immigrants that ventured to Tampa at the turn of the 19th century engendered a very rare breed of human being. Many of us are still living not too far from our birthplace in either West Tampa or Ybor City. Most of our old homes have vanished either through decay or destruction by an Urban Renewal program that wiped out many of the typical frame houses that were so unique to the cigar culture of Tampa. The program is now referred to as "Urban Removal" because nothing was built in their place for over 25 years. Back then, houses were built close to the cigar factories and rented to immigrant cigar makers but home ownership was not rare. There were a few who brought money over from the old country or saved enough here to buy homes.

The newcomers spoke only their native tongue and knew very little about this new country. As a matter of survival over the years they established societies patterned somewhat on those in their mother countries. Mutual benefit clubs were organized largely to provide medical care but other amenities were available such as theater, dances, sports, libraries and many other means of entertainment and enlightenment. The cantinas in the various clubs became a special place for men to play dominoes, cards, chess, smoke cigars, drink Cuban coffee, a shot of brandy, whiskey or beer and talk. The club buildings still stand and some are still active mostly as social clubs and repositories of the past. Much to the dismay of the oldsters, the younger generations became increasingly more "Americanized" and slowly weaned off the world of their parents.

The immigrants that came at the turn of the century could not have timed it worse. Not only did they have to endure the normal suffering associated with trying to eke out a living in a foreign country, but the worst depression in the history of the United States was just around the corner. My generation

(1930's) of "depression babies" became the bridge between the ways of the old country and the new.

Our parents and grandparents came to "the New World," (as my father called it) with inflated expectations about freedom and opportunity. Visions of El Dorado streets laden with gold, friendly cowboy types unfurling long welcome mats in a democratic society with justice, fair play and equality for all soon degenerated into stark realty. Freedom yes, but those other virtues were long in coming and had to be earned the hard way. Mostly poor uneducated farm or city laborers from countries with little roots in democracy, no educational opportunity and living under the thumb of a fading aristocracy gave the newcomers a Pollyanna attitude that magnified the disappointment when it inevitably came. That enormous let down resulted in a whole generation growing up with "something to prove." That old chip on our shoulders energized us. Our definition of justice was nothing more than the opportunity to prove that we were better. America's greatness lies in its system. Once my generation squeezed through at least nine years of school, it began to equalize itself and look "American."

Those of us "squeezing through" had a tough time doing so, but there was a silver lining associated with this ordeal. It produced some very interesting characters. Underdogs from birth, groveling for position was fundamental to us. Spanish, Sicilian and Cuban people were not exactly compatible, but some school teachers brought us closer when they looked down their noses at us. They (teachers) like many other "Americans" put us all in one convenient basket. We were all "Latins."

One of those "unforgettable" characters that so personified our dilemma and who continues to fortify my belief in the indomitable human will to survive was one of those people who went through life for the most part unnoticed.

Alfredo Guillermo Toroño was an insignificant, inconsequential member of a gang of ruffians who chased me home daily during my first months of public school. Alfredito (Little Alfred) was even smaller and skinnier than I. When he stood sideways he was almost invisible. The little guy was just trying to survive in a very hostile environment like all the rest of us "mojones." Alfredito seldom spoke and when he did he never said anything. His long, thin face, dark complexion, beak like nose, straight black hair, slanted eyes, high cheek bones and quiet demeanor tells me (now that I know better) that he was possibly Siboney Indian/Caucasian mix. At V.M. Ybor nobody knew anything about racial composition nor gave a damn.

The only time poor Alfredito got any notice was when the teacher found lice in his hair during the monthly "piojo hunt," and put him on public display in front of the class. Those who had the misfortune of harboring the little bugs were marched out to the hall and treated with boric acid powder. "*Piojo*" (lice) hunts were unannounced, but we knew when it was coming when we spotted the teacher putting on white gloves and pulling out a pair of wooden tongs from her desk drawer. Nobody wanted to be a "*piojoso*," dreaded carrier of the curse! In spite of all precautions, like washing your hair daily with cold water and Octagon soap, the pests persisted and flourished. There was no hot water unless you took the time to heat a bucket on the kerosene stove, besides it was considered unhealthy to wash your hair more than twice a week. The little bastards jumped from head to head, so at one time or another most of us were separated from the "cleans" and thrown in with the rest of the untouchables by a sneering teacher with a disgusted look on her face. Alfredito was a regular "untouchable."

Like most kids of that time, Alfredito was a gang member only because he was afraid not to. Maybe "gang" is not the correct classification for these loosely knit groups. Children clung to certain bullies for protection against other strong guys. Everybody was stronger than Alfredito.

Gang leaders seldom took issue with each other. These chiefs were satisfied to rule their own particular fiefdom and not too willing to chance losing a fight to one another. Our leader was "Chato," a burly older kid with a real stupid look on his face. The other liege lord was "Chino" whose three lumps on the back of his head distinguished him from other primates. One good look at these guys and you'd never doubt the Theory of Evolution. There were some odd balls who adhered to no gang. These independents were very strong physically with no ambition to rule, too dumb to know how or had a relative that everybody was scared of. Both Chato and Chino were "*piojosos*," and probably the major cause of the lice epidemic, but nobody told them so.

Alfredito spoke almost no English and very limited, bad Castilian. His family were very poor Cuban immigrants who, like most of ours, had come to work in the cigar factories. Over the years, I would often think of him, even though I never saw him again after V.M. Ybor. I guess it's because he was sort of an extreme version of what the rest of us were—frightened little people from another world just trying to survive. Many of us have either forgotten what it felt like or refuse to remember. I haven't. Alfredito was poorer and more afraid than the rest of us and embarrassed at being what he was. He stayed home from school for a whole week one time. Nobody knew where he lived, and because he would not tell the teacher why he was out, he got all unexcused absences. I found out through our undercover information system that he didn't have any shoes and didn't want anybody to make fun of him—especially in front of the girls.

Most took lunch to school. Anyone who bought lunch was considered well off. Nobody liked the lunches at school anyway and at ten cents a clip it was a bit steep. Alfredito's lunch was in his back pocket. It was a long piece of Cuban bread cut in half lengthwise filled with crushed garlic and used lard. Yes—a garlic and lard sandwich. The ugly chorizo sandwiches I often took were filet mignon for Alfred.

Breakfast for the lot of us was the traditional Cuban coffee with evaporated milk (fresh milk was unknown to me prior to World War II) and a piece of Cuban bread. That is still standard for many Ybor City and West Tampa natives. You can tell the difference between Ybor gentlemen and West Tampa 'colonials' by the way they dunk Cuban bread into their café con leche. Ybor Citians sink the bread only as deep their second knuckle.

With so spare a breakfast, we were all starving by ten a.m. That's when we were in Miss Barrow's Nature Studies class. Most teachers really tried to help us overcome our many hurdles. I went into teaching myself because of the wonderful ones I had throughout my school years. But there were a few who really didn't like us, often inferring that we were inferior and even suggesting that we should go back to "where we belong." Then there were some who were not as honest in their disdain, but we could sense their disgust. We were damned sure about Miss Barrow by the way she took extra care that none of us got near enough to touch her. I once overheard her referring to us as "those little roaches." That's why I often proudly refer to myself and others of my ilk as Ybor City Roaches. It's amazing that we didn't develop a worse inferiority complex than we did. None of us roaches really ever shook it off.

Nature Studies class was about two thirds gone and Miss Barrow was enthusiastically telling us about plants. She had drawn one on the board complete with roots, stems, leaves, and a big flower. With the gait and fire of an evangelist preacher, she pranced up and down the aisles with a long pointer, stopping now and then to ask one of her terrified listeners to repeat what she had just uttered. She always picked a boy, some poor slob who could hardly speak English so she could make fun of him—in front of the girls. We all wanted to be invisible. We looked like a pack of little mice, with bulging eyes waiting while the cat teased until devouring the unlucky.

Alfredito was so starved that he no longer cared about anything except the greasy banquet he was sitting on. His eyes had a transparent glaze over them and his lids were at half mast—product of another "no breakfast morning." The smell from the garlic had already penetrated his skull and in shear desperation, Alfredito's body took over his little brain and the pores on his buttocks were trying to consume the sandwich through the process of osmosis, which Miss Barrow was explaining. Sitting right next to him, I saw him slowly inch his left hand toward the sandwich tucked in his left back pocket. I knew what he was about to do. Eating in class was a capital offense. In Barrow's class there was no trial. The punishment—death by paddle in a public execution—in front of the girls!

The instrument of execution was a quarter inch-thick, foot-and-one-half long paddle with a thin handle and lettering that read "ICE CREAM." It was all one piece with eighth inch holes to provide little resistance to the surrounding atmosphere. "ICE CREAM" looked like the flap on a B-17 bomber! Barrow was enforcer, prosecutor, judge, jury and EXECUTIONER. Only time I saw her happy was when she caught some poor bastard committing a crime . . . like passing a pencil to a fellow peasant, whispering, talking or not sleeping when she ordered all 45 overactive kids to put their heads down between their folded arms and SLEEP! We had to fake it. One raised eyebrow—EXECUTION! Fred Sanchez was caught writing his girl's name on his desk!!! We never saw him again. Talk about bullying! Barrow was the Marquis de Sade of Bullying. She made "Chato" look like Florence Nightingale. Even "Chino" was scared shitless of her.

Barrow was in great shape. Paddling was an art for her. It was poetry in motion. The strokes were administered with diabolical precision on the buttocks, back of the thighs and (Aaaaaooooo!) calves with machine gun rhythm. Punishment continued as long as she deemed necessary depending on her energy level that day or whether the condemned cried out or moved. Wearing short pants to school was a bad, bad, bad idea. Girls seldom got beaten. I never saw one get it. They were always "good."

Alfredito's left hand had reached the sandwich. Eyes fixed on Barrow, like a snake stalking a rat, he put his bony fingers around the greasy wrapper and slowly pulled the sandwich out. His right arm served as decoy, placidly resting on top of his desk. With only his left hand available, Alfredito managed to halfway unwrap his lunch without making a sound. It was incredible. The grease had sound-proofed the normally noisy Cuban bread paper. In one blink of the eye, he pushed a quarter of the long sandwich into his mouth, tore off a chunk (I can still see his white teeth sinking into the crust) and shoved the remains into his back pocket. The attack had taken no more than three seconds. It was still close, Barrow's animal instincts caused her to turn quickly, almost trapping the mongoose. She starred at him as we both froze. No one else in the room knew what he and I knew. Alfredo puckered his lips and looked straight ahead in a courageous attempt to conceal the contents within his mouth. He had managed to put New York City into Largo and somehow swallowed the evidence by the time she blinked. It was like watching a pelican swallow a large catfish. The food hung around in the pouch momentarily, then unbelievably slid down the throat and into the gullet. She stopped talking, squinted her eyes, starred at him again for a moment, then continued her lecture.

Alfredito, the least among us, the super-underdog, the lowest roach in the food chain had beaten the system! Our eyes met. We both smiled ever slightly. It was a great moment—one great victory for the huddled masses.

As so often happens in life, success was too much for Alfredito to handle. I've seen some of the most successful people go under because they had poor sense of timing—they didn't know when to stop. It is the way of human nature I suppose. The garlic, lard and Cuban bread tort he swallowed whole only elevated his desperation for food and when I saw his left hand sneaking back to his oily pocket, I knew he was in trouble. Again he pulled the sandwich out. This time with the careless bravado that comes with success. The wrapper was still half open from the last assault. When he ferociously sank his teeth for another quarter sandwich, it was like watching a Great White attacking a young seal.

"Alfredito don't . . ." I yelled as the tyrant turned quickly. Trapped like rats. Not only did she see my little pal chomping down on the remains of his lunch, but she also caught me trying to warn him of the impending catastrophe. My blood curdled and a great cold settled in my stomach. Alfredito was charged with the heinous crime of eating his own grease and garlic in class and I was accessory after the fact in an act of treason. Aiding and abetting an enemy of the state. For Barrow it must have been the closest thing to the sexual experience she probably never had.

All those fans of quick justice that I encounter so often who attack civil rights guarantees, trial by jury and due process would have rejoiced in this case. Reprisal was instant, much to the pleasure of the executioner, and, not surprisingly, to many of my fellow roaches who now had some measure of comic relief in their otherwise lousy existence. Even the few who felt some sympathy were relieved somewhat. They constituted the "better them than us" group which is where Alfredo and I belonged.

We were marched before the class. She then picked up the mushy, smelly remnants of Alfredo's lunch with a pair of wooden tongs she used to check our hair for lice and threw it into the trash can as she held her nose with pompous indignation.

I was first. She turned me around roughly, pulled my short pants to the left to lessen the thin cloth's protection of my butt and then beat the hell out of me with that paddle. She was in great shape. Gleefully, she banged away. Back of the thighs hurt most then the calves till the back of my legs were marked blood red. My face was just as red, my eyes filled with tears as I concentrated on a large picture of George Washington hanging above the black board. I wouldn't blink in order to keep the tears from running down my cheeks. I kept thinking of that old Spanish saying that papa always recited when I was about to cry, "Miguel, los hombres no lloran." (Michael, men do not weep.) It wasn't the beating, painful as it was, it was the injustice—the indignity—in front of the class—in front of the girls.

It wasn't over. She made me stand facing the audience, some already snickering. I hated them and I hated her for doing this to me.

Alfredito's lips still shining from the lard he had consumed, was horrified. He had been standing next to me during the beating and heard my muffled moans (so the girls wouldn't hear.) With a diabolical, Barrymore grin on her face, she pointed at the "ICE CREAM" paddle. "Chocolate, vanilla, or strawberry?" she asked. Alfredo, forcing a smile meekly replied, "I no likee ice cream, sank you." The class roared.

Alfred had long pants, but it didn't matter. She pounded him unmercifully. The strokes made a different sound this time. Alfredo being even skinnier than I, the whacks hit more bone than flesh making them sound like a hammer hitting concrete. He held tears back as well as he could, but some escaped down his gaunt cheeks, greasy mouth and chin. He got it much worse than I. When totally exhausted, she finally stopped, made us stand facing the class for what seemed an eternity then ordered us into the cloak room for the remainder of the period. When all the class left for lunch at the sound of the bell, she made us wait while she powdered her long nose and painted her thin lips in a futile attempt to look pretty. I have no idea why, but when we looked at each other in the darkness of the cloakroom, our bodies still stinging from the "*golpes*" (blows) received, we started laughing right through the tears that now flowed freely and without shame. It was the joy of having survived. Our laughter became uproarious when I stuck my front tooth out, twisted my mouth to the right, made my lips look thin and said, "you little roaches" in a pretty good impersonation of "Madame de Sade." Alfredito laughed his burning ass off. We ate my lunch (a sardine and onion sandwich) that was pretty oily too. It was tough cutting the thing in half without a knife but we managed to do it under the shade of an old water oak that still lives near the back entrance of the school.

Both of us hid the terrible black and blue marks that adorned our legs and posteriors. Never told our mothers. We didn't want our Spanish-speaking mamas embarrassing us further. What went on in school was our business alone. No PTA, no "Welcome Parents Days," no complaints—no nothing.

The following day we're back in Nature Studies class. It was third period just before lunch. Miss Barrow is pleasantly talkative, almost sparkling. It wasn't too long before we knew why. Our principal, Mr. McLoughlin, was making the monthly rounds checking to see that "*las cucarachas*" (we roaches) were getting some sort of instruction. Barrow had pulled out her very best picture of a grasshopper and instead of the B-17 flap, she was using a more civilized, long pointer with a very red tip. She had just gone over the various parts of the grasshopper's body except for the rectum which in those days did not exist. We knew better because we had squashed many around the house. When Mr. McLoughlin appeared suddenly at the door she beamed like a blue/white spotlight.

"Children, please," she said, raising her arms for all to stand.

"What do we say when Mr. McLoughlin honors us with his presence?"

Right on cue we all said in musical unison, "Good morning to you, good morning to you, good morning, Mr. McLoughlin, good morning to you." He said, "thank you" and told Sunflower to continue.

With elevated enthusiasm, Miss Barrow spewed forth brilliantly, repeating what she had already covered. She then surprised us all by doing something she had never done before. She smiled broadly and asked, "Are there any questions?" Everybody was petrified. Who in the hell is going to ask anything about anything in front of the class, the tyrant and the principal? Besides, none of us (not even the girls) could speak English very well.

"Are there any questions," she repeated knowing that there'd be none from her potpourri of Latin morons. Sure that she had impressed Mr. Wonderful, the lord and master of the manor, she bid him adieu. "Wait," said the lord, "the little young man in back has his hand up." All heads turned toward the dummy row in back. It was Alfredito's tiny brown hand sticking up and even waving. It was astonishing! Is it possible, that this dumb bastard has not yet learned?

Barrow was totally aghast. With the principal observing this wonderful breakthrough however, she nodded as if this was the norm. She must have thought, "Is it possible that I have actually penetrated the infinitesimal brain of this Ybor City banana dock roach?"

She smiled subtly with the aura of a triumphant Joan of Arc, pointed at Alfredito and (without Anglicizing his name this time) in perfect Castilian said, "Alfredo?"

Every eye was on the demure Alfredito Guillermo Toroño who defiantly stood up straight, swallowed hard, took a very deep breath and said, "Meees, meeees, meeeeees Barrow, why ju no let me eat my sang-wicheee?"

Ybor City "roaches." (left to right): Louie Lopez, Tony Munoz, Charlie Gustaveson (El Craca), Me and Ernest Carrera. Photo taken near tobacco field barn near Windsor, Ct. Farm owner had the cojones (audacity) to hire this bunch of bottom feeders.

Chapter Four

"Hay Toros"

"Ah, for the good old days."

Familiar lamentation among those of my generation and unquestionably a good indication that we are approaching "geezerdom."

When you really stop to think about it, those "good old days" were not so good. Really, the good thing about the good old days is that we were young. The rest was spotty at best. It seems that nature makes it easier for us to remember the positive experiences and forget most of the bad or at least pull what's unsavory way back in our sub-conscience. I hear my generation so often moan about today's kids. They have no respect, they dress horribly, listen to nonsensical music which of course all leads to loose morality and consequent violent behavior. Ah, for the good old days!

Days of my youth flash before me every time I see a school bus loading kids. The difference between the behavior of the children today and those of my genre is truly astonishing. How moving it is to see a line of boys and girls neatly entering the bus one by one. No pushing, no shoving, no insults, no fighting—an orderly procession of little people about to be transported to an institution of learning. It is a sight that fills me with emotion. My two son's and my grandchildren's elementary school experiences were generally devoid of any conflagration or threats of violence. The fruits of peace, tranquility and order was theirs as cool, mild mannered teachers watched over them. Their problems with violent behavior came much later and very rarely. As the song says, "too few to mention." I taught high school for about seven years and can say without reservation that I never had a serious discipline problem.

These pastoral scenes are in stark contrast to my years in elementary school where orderly lines were possible only by the Gestapo tactics of teachers armed with wooden paddles to keep us from beating, kicking and elbowing each other for first place. I can only imagine the inevitable combat that would have ensued if we had been left to govern ourselves while entering a bus to go anywhere! There was no such thing as a school bus. You got to school however you could. Even the Gestapo could not control the savage charge toward the lunch room at the sound of the bell. The Horde of Genghis Khan in full gallop had nothing on my seventh grade (7B-2) at Washington Jr. High. I'll never forget the look on a substitute librarian's face when the lunch bell rang as she courageously tried to read us a story. Class emptied in a sixteenth of a second leaving her aghast with book in hand and index finger pointing to the ceiling as she was emphasizing a phrase. Only other person left in the room was a kid named Nilo who sat in his seat with eyes at half mast and a silly smile on his face after being hit on the back of the head with a dictionary.

Somehow most of us managed to get civilized. In spite of all the problems, we owe a great debt to public school in this great nation where every single human being is guaranteed an education. Public school or the "free school" as we called it is the most important institution in our democracy because without a relatively enlightened citizenry self government is impossible. To immigrant children it had yet another measure of importance. It was the bridge that made possible the crossing from the old world of our parents to the new world—America. Public school remains the great "Americanizer" of us all.

More important than good teachers and curriculum was the interfacing of people of various cultures, income and social levels thrown together and forced to deal with their differences. That's the real advantage of public school. Kids learn more from each other than from teachers. It is America's greatest virtue. It's what separates us from other systems.

By the time I got out of elementary school, I was less 'different' than my classmates, which included a few token "crackers" (a "craca" was anybody that was not a "Latin".) When finishing my ninth year (junior high class of 1947) I was the most educated (not wisest) person in my family and almost civilized. When I received my high school diploma I saw my father weep for the first time.

Old man Salvador saw in me the final step of my metamorphosis. I spoke and even looked like my cracker brethren much as I would never admit it. Who would have said then that in one single generation the son of immigrant cigar makers would wind up teaching in the very high school he had graduated from a scant 13 years earlier. That achievement would have been impossible anywhere but in America.

The "Americanization" of Joaquin Eugenio Espinosa was in its advanced stages in just 12 years. More important than overcoming the language barrier, learning numbers, science and history was the tolerance I ultimately developed for all people however different than I. Life-long friends more family than acquaintances are my greatest treasure and a major reason I live in Tampa. Although Jim Crow kept us segregated from our African brothers and sisters, the prejudice I endured and the lessons I learned from it made me an ardent supporter of the civil rights movement later. Early in my childhood my family spoke often of the terrible injustices suffered by African Americans in the United States. Spanish immigrants knew nothing of the American Civil War, Reconstruction, the Klan or Jim Crow.

The friends I made during those early years are much like friends made in foxholes. Perhaps comparing my childhood and adolescence to war is somewhat of an exaggeration, but being part Andalusian, a "Curro," gives me license to get away with some exaggeration. Forced to live together in school for some seven hours each weekday, sons and daughters of Spanish, Cuban and Sicilian immigrants were compelled to establish some sort of social accord in order to deal with each other and with the few "American" kids scattered throughout the school. The "cracas" in elementary school were easily made friends largely because they were too few to threaten us. Imagine how they felt! That cocoon we lived in almost totally segregated from the "Anglo" world we would later enter served as a great anchor, a fortress, a comfort for the rest of our lives. Ybor City and our colony, West Tampa, will always be home. It's what gives its natives that mysterious uniqueness that I call "salsa." I have known thousands of people and their offspring for a lifetime.

The Anglos (everybody that wasn't us) including almost all of our teachers, referred to us as "Latins," a designation that exists to this day as though our distinct cultures were all the same. Many "outsiders" called us all Cubans. We committed the same error by calling all others "*Americanos*" or Anglos or "crackers."

Cubans and Spaniards, although sharing the language and some customs, were very different and often not too fond of each other in those days. There had been a long and bloody struggle for Cuban independence from Spain at the end of the 19th Century. Tampa played a major role in the resulting Spanish-American War and the residue of that terrible conflict lingered throughout the early 20th Century. Spain's feeble grip on the Western Hemisphere held since 1492 was finally broken. Losing its very last colony, "the Pearl of the Antilles" was the final blow to the pride of my conquistador ancestors. Cigar factories in Tampa were either owned or managed by Spaniards, creating a serious schism between Spanish management and Cuban labor. Spanish supervisors often discriminated against Cuban and Sicilian applicants for jobs in the factories and for better paying or easier work. The air of aristocracy brought over from Spain even among former peasants was repulsive to Cuban and Sicilian workers. When the Spanish Civil War broke out an even greater division occurred. Now Spaniards with the Republic as well as many Cubans opposed other Spaniards who quietly favored the Fascist Franco. Many supported the Communists, which they believed was the party of the worker. All this was reflected in the children who lived it at home and in school. Americans in Tampa's power structure and other citizens were not exactly fond of all this and viewed anyone that spoke Spanish with suspicion of being subversive or even a spy.

These great issues had somewhat died down by the time I became old enough to be seriously affected by them but I got a good taste of it at home. With a Spanish father, a mother born in a thatched roof house in Cuba of Spanish/Irish immigrants and a host of tenants and friends with adamantly vocal opinions gave me a rare opportunity to benefit from the discussions that ensued. Born in 1931 my first encounters with heated debate occurred in the ample front porches that we enjoyed on 11th Avenue in Ybor City. All current affairs were food for argument but the biggy was the Spanish Civil War.

In the Sicilian community, smallest of the Ybor minorities, things were very different. They even spoke another language and had little to say about the problems of Spanish-speaking people. Although a hard laboring class at first this unique immigration became small business owners (shoe repair, clothing, groceries and other.) some wisely invested their meager resources in land on the outskirts of Tampa farming vegetables and raising cattle. Others went to work in cigar factories. Many nationally renown produce, grocery and diary companies are the direct result of the hard-working, tenacious Sicilian families of those days. Sicilian kids were the first in significant numbers to break into the professions such as teaching, medicine, law and engineering. Often ridiculed for being tight with money and eating macaroni with no sauce, those sacrifices paid well for their offspring. The few Latin teachers that I encountered in my early years were Sicilian. My very first love was with my fourth grade teacher at V.M. Ybor Elementary, Millie Randazzo. I owe a great debt of gratitude to her and to Ms. Salice (never knew her first name) for the kindness and understanding they showed me when I needed it most. They understood the isolation and loneliness that a non-English speaking, skinny, long nosed totally ignored kid felt.

A fourth minority interfaced with us not as neighbors but through business contact. They were a small scattering of Jewish merchants that owned clothing, furniture, linoleum floor covering, and kitchen utensil stores on Seventh

Avenue (*La Septima*). Contact with their children came later in junior and high schools since most of them lived in Tampa Heights just west of the Ybor line. They were established families already in tune with American society and been in the professions and business for generations. We got along very well with them in spite of the economic and cultural differences. Out similarity was in the discrimination that existed against our kind.

African-Americans and Afro-Cubans were not part of our "Americanization." Jim Crow kept us apart. I had no black friend until my show business years in the late fifties. Although there was a Marti-Maceo organization for Cuban whites and blacks, contact was rare and Afro-Cubans had a terrible time. There was no room for them among whites or among American blacks because of their significant cultural differences. It is indeed a sad chapter in the story of Tampa.

The differences among the three "Latin" groups were eventually tolerated by each of the factions, but things did get a bit testy during those early years. Parents of Spanish or Sicilian youngsters were particularly opposed to marriages outside their own kind. Cubans were a bit more liberal about such things probably because they had recently fought an entrenched Spanish colonial aristocracy to gain independence much as the Americans had against their English forefathers.

Sicilians held to the medieval custom of keeping the wealth within the family and choosing a favorite son (not daughter) to entrust leadership roles in the family's affairs. Marriage outside these boundaries was a first class taboo, enough to disown and disinherit an offspring. Similar among Spanish families with perhaps a little more tolerance. A few Spanish families sent their kids to higher education, but most expected their kids to go to work as soon as they were old enough. All my brothers were working full time right out of junior high. In graduated from high school but my brothers and I had been working while attending school since age eight or nine.

These old customs faded rather dramatically by the outbreak of World War II and by the time my generation reached puberty we fell in love and married whomever we pleased including "Crackers" whom we began to encounter in increasing numbers as schools drew students from wider geographic areas.

With all these differences it is indeed a miracle that we got along as well as we did but compared to the world my sons and grandchildren faced, ours was a combat zone. Fights were a matter of routine all the way through my ninth grade. Schools being the focal point where kids gathered, it was there that most fights occurred. The same can be said of dances, parties, sports events and other social activities. Most slugfests at George Washington Jr. High School were pre-arranged for after school where the girls would not see anybody lose, but fights would flare up in the halls, rest rooms or (although rarely) in class. When a main event was pending, usually between two real tough guys, the show was ballyhooed for hours or even days at a time. Sometimes the differences between the belligerents had been settled through an apology or negotiations, but the publicity forced them to battle anyway because neither wanted to be accused of "yellowing out." On the day of the showdown, the word went out, "*hay toros*"—bullfights today! Announcements were made in Spanish so teachers would not catch on. They of course knew what was going on but as long as it was after school they would not interfere with our way of settling disputes.

Combat was attended to inside a human ring with belligerents fighting in the middle. The ring moved automatically with the fighters who duked it out until there was a knockout or a surrender. Most times they would stop by mutual consent when both felt they'd had enough. There was some semblance of justice in these trials by combat. If one of the contenders was much smaller than his opponent, a family member or close friend of more formidable size or experience could be substituted if the other side agreed.

Cause for most antagonism was a cultural slur about your clan, moving in on what you assumed was your girl (most times she was unaware that she was somebody's girl) throwing your lunch away or stealing it. Touching your butt "*tocandome el culo*" or any mention or derogatory remark about your mother resulted in instant reprisal no matter where it happened. It meant that the other guy wants a fight for sure! Anything derogatory uttered by a "cracker" resulted in immediate violence unless you were outnumbered at which time you fled and came back with your guys.

As we got older, fights were less common but more dangerous as we got bigger and stronger (not me). Those were the times when it was "us Latins" against them "crackers." Many encounters were at football games and at favorite handouts for a particular high school. Hillsborough kids hung out at Milian's, my gang (Jefferson High) at Falor's and Plant High at The Colonnade (still there.) For me the most violent point of encounter was the old Tourist Club in Sulphur Springs. The building remains to this day (2005) right next to the Hillsborough River bridge on Nebraska Avenue. Those Seminole Heights and Sulphur Springs "crackers" were tough as hell and mean as us. I surmise that their sour disposition was associated with the fact that most of them were as poor as us and nobody wanted to be at the bottom of the ladder. We didn't' know much about them and they didn't know much about us. Any one of us caught alone in their territory was in for a rough time and the same was true for them in our domain. When we did have the temerity to go to each others fiefdom, it was in groups of ten or more. My nightmare was to find myself alone in one of those foreign lands. I could usually get away with it if I kept my mouth shut, but strangers in these alien environs were always looked upon with mistrust. Sooner or later some tough guy would ask you something like, "You ain't one 'o them God-damned Cubans, are you?"

Old Sulphur Springs Tourist Club building whence I jumped into the Hillsborough River to keep from getting more golpes (beatings). I took this photo from a boat in recent years, lest we forget.

We had made a very bad habit of going to the Tourist Club dances about every other month on Friday or Saturday nights. Invariably, "*golpes*" (beatings) ensued. Rightly so. After all, we were actually dancing with "their" women! It was war. Even with the support of my gang, I generally got my ass kicked pretty good being 15 years old, about 5 ft. 6 inches tall and weighing in at about 118 pounds—wet! To put it mildly, I was not exactly a menace. Like Daffy Duck, I was a feeder animal and had to use more wit than brawn to manage survival. My courage consisted of two or three shots of Corbys whiskey and my tactic was "hit and run." Nonetheless, with guys like Louie Lopez, Tony Munoz, Jack De la Llana, Jaime Gonzalez and sure-fire knockout puncher, Tony Marchese, I had a good chance of staying out of the Gonzalez Clinic.

Munoz and Lopez were more or less like me, but De la Llana, Gonzalez and Marchese were the ass-kickers. They were a little older and all three had been working lifting heavy feed sacks, auto repairing and woodcutting. Marchese was born on 5th Avenue in Ybor City. His father had a saw mill on the small property. Legend has it that as soon as Tony could walk, his father put a hand saw in his right hand and told him to start cutting wood. After 15 years, Tony's right arm was a Sicilian mallet. Combined with a violent disposition, Marchese was a formidable weapon to have on your side. Being short and a little chubby made him appear deceivingly vulnerable. It was the perfect trap. He loved to allow big guys to push him about a bit and call him "shorty" and "guap" while he positioned his little fat body sideways, cock his shotgun arm and fix his cold blue eyes on the chin. The look on his face was frightening as every ounce of his energy went to the mallet. The thunderous shot to the unsuspecting chin was a thing of beauty. That surprised, torpid look on the faces of those big bullies as their listless bodies tumbled down was worth any beating I may have received in the conflagrations that followed.

It was the Monday morning after a particularly violent Saturday at the Tourist Club that Mr. Catron, a substitute ninth grade science teacher, noticed that my nose was leaning a bit to the right, more crimson that usual and my upper lip cracked and swollen. Together with the dark circles under both eyes, I looked like raccoon road kill.

"What the shit happened to you?" he said. "You been sorting wildcats?" It wasn't very funny. I liked Mr. Catron because no other teacher spoke to me in that kind of "grown-up" vernacular and because he had been a fighter pilot in the war. He flew P-40's in North Africa! That made him some kind of God. I loved airplanes. I explained that during a "Hay Toros" free-for-all I had been hit with a chair and then cold-cocked while I was kicking a downed enemy in the ribs with my pointed Tom McAnn shoes.

"Hot damn," he drawled, "You sure got your ass kicked real bad. Did you do any damage?" Embarrassed I told him that I never inflicted much injury. I had no weight behind my punches. I'd pepper my opponents, but never with enough force to knock anybody out.

"Are you accurate enough to put your fist on their chin?"

When I replied in the affirmative, he closed one eye and looked hard at me with the open one as he put a roll of pennies in my minuscule right hand.

"Hit somebody on the chin with this as hard as you can and you'll knock piss outa him."

Just then it dawned on me. Here's about as red-necked a cracker as you could find and he is giving me, an Ybor City "guap", advice on how to knock out a cracker! Maybe Papa was right, "*Americanos*" are a just and democratic people. That adage was not always true, but it sure was in Mr. Catron's case. I never forgot that lesson. I've since judged people one at a time.

I took the role of pennies, but I didn't use them for his purpose. I spent the pennies on a Milky Way and when I saw my grandfather, Jose, cutting a piece of iron pipe to fix a faucet I asked him to cut me two pieces long enough to fit the width of my fists. It was perfect.

The following Saturday I took a bus to Sulphur Springs wearing my brothers zoot suit and my new "*zapatos de charol*" that shined enough to blind a hawk. Charol shoes were the cheapest imitation leather footwear you could buy. My friend Tony Munoz used to tell me that if you stood still over wet ground wearing those shoes they'd grow roots. Nonetheless they would serve my purpose for at least a while since my Thom McAns had holes bigger than doughnuts. I had "word of honor" assurance that my gang (featuring Marchese and Jaimie) would meet me there early. I would have never ventured into "Suffering Springs" without that guarantee. There were better ways of dying.

I walked into the club with the confident look of a raccoon after sex. First rule was to never show fear. It excites the sharks. I walked in without looking at anyone at the bar, put my foot defiantly on the rail and ordered a shot of Corby's just as though I belonged there. Three shots of Corby's and you start looking like the parrot on the label! After my third I looked around as the bartender poured number four. At 35 cents a pop, I had to watch my extravagance. I might have to buy some drinks to keep the natives friendly. I nonchalantly checked my pockets to make sure Catron's weapons of mass destruction were still there.

No sign of my guys and I began to get concerned when a cracker that was longer than a day without a drink wearing a very black motorcycle jacket and a visor cap with a snake emblem on it started eyeing me two stools over. Little by little he slid over towards me till he stood right next to me. Finally in a very deep voice he says, "Hey shit head, we don't allow Cuban niggers in this bar." As my bowels loosened, I looked once more to see if help was near. No sign!

Like a cornered rat I figured there was no way out of this without "*golpes*" (beatings) upon my skinny ass. Amazing how quickly you can size things up when there are few options. I thought of using my mercurial speed and haul ass. That was quickly eliminated when a quick glance indicated that three guys with nasty grins were at the only entrance (and exit) to the second floor dance hall. Perhaps a spirited dash to the women's rest room. They wouldn't follow me there. Would they? Forget it. Besides, the windows were too small even for my reptilian derriere. There were better ways to die than to be flushed down a Tourist Club toilet! Then it came. My Angel hit me right between the horns with the only way out. A long row of windows line the south side of the dance hall directly across from the bar. They were all open to cool the second floor with the fragrant breezes of the Hillsborough River fresh after the benediction of sewage engendered from recent May rains.

A dash across the floor and a jump into the river was about it. What about my shoes? Cheap, imitation charol (more like reinforced cardboard) but they were brand new. I chose to slip them off (no laces) then hold them over my head with left hand while I paddled across the river with my right. All this I figured in a matter of seconds.

The big guy pushed against me again. "You still here, shorty?" His pals were all laughing across the bar. "Looks like he's scared shitless and can't move," said the bald-headed bartender. When I said I didn't want "no trouble" they howled.

S-l-o-o-o-w-l-y I reached into the right pocket of my coat and gripped the thin piece of pipe as I turned my upper torso slightly to the right. My back was towards the bar so the laughing hyenas could not notice my hand slipping into the pocket. Now my left shoulder pointed toward the open jaw—still laughing. I cocked my right arm, turned my head toward the target and there it was big as a pelican's beak. I could not miss it. But could I put enough weight behind the dart to get my first knockout? "Let it be now, God, let it be now." My little fist led the rest of my 118 pounds right into the jaw. I had put my jock strap into the shot. I was later told that I looked like an arrow flung out of a 60-pound bow. The man looked at me. His laughter had come to an abrupt stop and his eyes opened wide with a look of total shock and bewilderment. Oh no, NO KNOCKOUT! Before I took my first step, he grabbed my left shoulder with his right hand. It felt like a ton. Here it is—time for my usual "golpeadura." Suddenly his grip loosened, his eyes rolled back and he began to fall. It was like watching the demolition of a skyscraper when the bottom implodes and the structure falls neatly into a pile of rubbish—like the wicked witch disappearing into a puddle—like King Kong falling off the Empire State Building. It was magnificent. An unforgettable moment. I've played it back in my mind a thousand times in slow motion.

Finally realizing what had happened, I put two more punches into the falling building and when it fell to the floor, I kicked it several times on the ribs with my little pointed chorol "zapaticos." I had turned into a savage and almost forgot my tenuous position.

I quickly slipped off my shoes before Goliath's comrades could realize the unbelievable event they had just witnessed, flew across the floor and jumped out of an open window into the refreshing waters of the Hillsborough River. The gathering at the bar didn't think I'd jump. They looked down from the second story, yelled invectives and threw beer bottles at me. "Sucker punch," they bellowed. Even if I had been hit with a bottle—nothing—nothing— could take the glory of that moment from me as I paddled across the river with my right hand while holding my shoes out of the water with my left.

My delight took a back seat to survival instincts when I saw the gang led by Goliath running across the Nebraska Avenue bridge hoping to intercept me as I got to the other side. After some trouble negotiating the rocks on the bank I got back on "*terra firma*." Once I had some traction under my bare feet, my ordeal was over. All those crackers saw for a very short time was my ass and my elbows. After a two block chase down old 15th Street they gave up and by the time I got to Hillsborough Avenue I was bone dry from the wind my speed generated.

My gang showed up after I had taken leave and got beaten up pretty badly, but Marchese knocked out Goliath again. I would like to tell him that I had softened him up! It was indeed a rare pleasure to relate the story to my dear cracker teacher, Mr. Catron who made that dream come true. It's never happened again.

About a month later I went back to the Tourist Club. This time with my entourage in case of another "*hay toros*" free-for-all. It didn't happen but I saw the bartender twisting his mouth to one side as he wiped the bar with a white towel and telling some guy on the other side, "Don't mess around with that little skinny son of a bitch with the long nose, he's a professional boxer!"

Brother Lionel Carreno, for whom I served as "war correspondent," translating letters so he and my mother could communicate during the war years.

Chapter Five

It's War!

Great events that change the course of history were commonplace in the lifetime of my generation. Volumes are written about The Great Depression, World War II, Korea, Cold War, Civil Rights Movement; assassinations of President John F. Kennedy, Robert Kennedy, Dr. Martin Luther King, Jr. and the Vietnam War. The two wars in Iraq will undoubtedly have a sizeable impact. We'll have to wait for that final outcome. No generation in the history of the United States has had so many life-altering events, each having a profound and lasting effect on those of us who suffered through them. Those conscious of what was happening and survived those tumultuous times made for a very tough genre of skeptics.

War is probably the most disruptive and painful of all the evils that can befall man. In our case World War II and Korea represents the toll on the final bridge toward acceptance by American "firsters" who thought the country was exclusively theirs. It was a very high tariff paid in blood and grief. All immigrants from Indians to English to Irish to "Latinos" to African-Americans have had to suffer through war to earn acceptance which still came slowly. African-Americans, even though living here longer than most, still had to wait for the Civil Rights Movement of the 60's to stand with the rest of us as first-class citizens. Mexican-Americans are going through it now in Iraq. Santayana was right, history repeats itself because man is too ignorant to learn it.

The other arena in which differences are readily acceptable is sports. As long as your team wins, it no longer matters who is on it. Uniforms moved us toward equality and justice even if reason didn't. Those uniforms worn by boys of all colors and cultural background did a lot to start the ball rolling. Our guys came back from war proud of their ancestors and feeling just as American as anybody else. My brother Lionel returned after four years in combat zones with a very nasty attitude and no longer timid about his vowel-ending name. Parents of those kids wounded and the many who died in defense of the only country they knew were no longer ready to take a back seat to anybody. Baldomero Lopez, Congressional Medal of Honor posthumous recipient, threw himself over a live hand grenade to save his squad. He showed no concern for race or national origin of those for whom he gave his last full measure.

My own personal loss is the death of Eugene (Sonny) Fernandez, my godfather's oldest son who died in the invasion of Normandy. The Fernandez's lived next door to us on 11th Avenue. He was one of my brother Hector's closest friends. I can still remember their enthusiasm when they boarded the train at Union Station. It was traditional for close friends to send off new recruits with a special dinner at the Spanish Park Restaurant. Children were never invited to these things but as usual, my big brother wouldn't leave me out. I remember it well because it's the first time I had experienced split pea soup. As it turned out, my brother's arthritis attack during basic training was so severe that he was medically discharged. We had not heard a word from him in weeks while he suffered in a Georgia army hospital. His hands were so cramped that he couldn't write. It saved his life. Much to our eternal grief, Sonny was healthy enough to lose it all in Normandy.

It's hard to believe that the war lasted just four years. The span of time between a 10 year-old and 14 makes an enormous difference. Those years are very long indeed. They are the first part of that long, long journey between childhood and manhood. I thought the war would never end. Unaware back then, now I realize that with three brothers in uniform, my home was very tense. Now I understand why mama never showed much concern. Kept her anguish inside to keep me happy. War, war, war! It was everywhere at all times. There was no other news. People depended on radio and newspapers. Any visual was at least a week old in movie newsreels. Now we know that most of the information was censored. We were always winning or about to win. News coverage of the war was what the government allowed in order to keep civilian morale up and productive.

Those too old, unfit, or successful draft-dodgers that stayed behind had full employment, lots of money but little to buy. Inflation was rampant and black markets prosperous. No new cars, food (butter, meats, eggs, sugar etc.) gasoline and other items were rationed all sacrificed for the war effort. It was total war and total support for the armed forces. We knew exactly why we were fighting and who the enemy was. Everybody was involved in one way or another. Many worked two jobs. Opportunity languished everywhere as Tampa, already a two air base city (Drew Field and MacDill) became an important ship-building center. Our major shopping, recreation centers and especially U.S.O. facilities were loaded with service men from all over the U.S. Dances at the Cuban Club, Centro Asturiano and especially the Matinee Dances at the Centro Espanol were full of uniformed guys from all the services. This bothered some of our locals who were not too fond of "outsiders" coming in and taking "their" girls. Uniforms have a special appeal. By and large, most locals got along with the soldiers and many remained in Tampa or came back after the war to marry girls they couldn't forget. Besides, our guys were in some other community going through the same thing.

Movies, even cowboy westerns and cartoons were about the war. Beaches were blacked out—no street lights to avoid silhouetting tankers that may be torpedoed right off our Gulf Coast! Comic strips and magazines like Captain Marvel (my guy) Batman, Spy Smasher and Blue Beetle all dealt with Nazi or Japanese spies and other war related themes. Signs all over warned that "Loose lips sink ships." Or "Is this trip really necessary?" with Uncle Sam pointing his long finger at you trying to keep us in tune with the war effort. The drone of B-17 bombers stationed at Drew Field flew overhead day after day practicing bomb runs and landings. They flew so low over my house on Ybor Street that I felt I could hit them with a rock. The old frame house shook to its foundation as they roared overhead—grim reminders that we were in a fight to the finish.

Along with being an ardent model airplane builder, I belonged to the "Junior Commandos" of the Ponce de Leon Housing Project. We became expert in identifying enemy aircraft, even Italian war planes! We were so stupid that we never realized that none of those had enough range to cross either ocean. No matter, war is war! My responsibility, together with Joe Torano and Jack Gonzalez was to patrol the parking lot and watch out for thieves sifting gasoline out of cars or possible spies in the area. Any "suspicious" activity was to be reported to the housing project office. I and my pal Jack were so dedicated to the case that we donned masks and capes and clandestinely watched for spies and other sorts from top of an oak tree next to the parking lot! The only spy that we caught was a man who was hiding in some bushes and then sneaking into an apartment after the woman's husband had left. A Nazi spy meeting for sure. The suspicious activity was duly reported by the caped crusaders. Our thorough investigation, including times in and out by several suspects and complete descriptions of the culprits led to some severe beatings and a scandal talked about for years. One of the "spies" who met each evening with enemy agents happened to be married to an employee at the housing project office. We were promptly taken off the case and reassigned as enemy aircraft spotters. War is hell!

My innocence about the war came to an abrupt stop when I learned that Sonny Fernandez had been killed. The Fernandez family is one of the most important influences in my life. Like all genuinely virtuous people, they are unaware of the good they do. Head of the household was my father's closest friend, Eugenio (Eu-ye) Fernandez, my godfather. Modest, conservative in dress and manner, wise, well-informed, patient and understanding, I never heard him raise his voice yet no one doubted his authority. His children, Sonny (Eugene) Albert (Berti) Geraldine (Nini) and the baby, Robert (Robertico) were sterling. Berti served in the navy till the end of the war. Matriarch, Natalia and everybody's grandmother, Eugenia, were heaven-sent angels as were two aunts Maria Teresa "Cucha" and Mercedes. As it was in those days, all lived harmoniously in a large house. Eugenio was a bookkeeper and office manager at the Santaella Cigar Factory in West Tampa for as long as I can remember. Better off financially than most of us, he had a car that he used to go to work and once in a while take the family out for a ride (un raqui.) Every summer they spent a month in Clearwater Beach, another rarity in those days. For me, they were Ybor City's answer to the Judge Hardy family portrayed in movies—so different from my own. Not a single one of those Fernandez's ever flaunted their good fortune. Not a one of us felt anything but affection for them all. Down to earth and democratic, their behavior evoked absolutely no envy by anyone. Every birthday "Eu-ye" unceremoniously slipped me a five dollar bill when no one was looking. A "fin" back in the late 30's was a small fortune. Their front porch was the center of my universe. Sitting on the concrete steps I listened to a bi-lingual dialogue among the educated, less educated and uneducated. Eugenio, well-read and wise, never imposed his knowledge. He shared it painlessly with all, listened much and spoke sparingly.

For years I returned to that porch to visit the family. As soon as possible, I took my children there in hope that they may experience a semblance of what it once was. There was a warmth there that I cannot explain. A feeling of comfort, of belonging. It reinforced awareness of who I was and where I belonged. An indispensable piece of knowledge that I've carried with me throughout the years. Difficult to understand why such good people would be so ill-fated to lose a beloved son. It was indeed a dark chapter in the lives of so many families in our community. Burned into my memory is the horror on the faces of folks sitting on their porches when the Western Union telegram boy turned his bicycle onto your street. A freckled-faced kid in a baggy uniform with a pencil stuck into his cap turned into the angel of death bringing notice that a loved one had been killed, missing or wounded. "United States

Department of War regrets to inform you that . . . . Holding our breath we prayed, "please, don't put the mark of death on my door." Enough tears were shed to make the Hillsborough River a twin. What is worse Korea, Vietnam, Iraq, and Afghanistan awaited the children and grandchildren of that "greatest generation" who fought and died so heroically "so my kids won't have to" they said. What have we done?

Staff Sgt. Lionel Carreno served in the 807th U.S. Army Aviation Battalion from June 1940 to October 1945 in the Pacific War theater, Aleutians, Iwo Jima and Okinawa combat zones.

Chapter Six

War Correspondent

My oldest half brother, Lionel Carreno, had joined the Army before the Second World War broke out. A very good auto mechanic and general handyman, he was assigned to the Engineer Corp and shipped out (left from MacDill Field by rail) in June, 1940—destination Alaska. A chronic asthmatic, an assignment to that "ice box" appeared to be a death sentence. He had married a pretty girl just moved across the street from our home a couple of months before he was shipped out. His young wife, the former Anita Torres, was to live with us for "just a little while," not more than a year. None of us dreamed of the catastrophe that was just around the corner. Dec. 7 of that year changed everything. We didn't see him again (except in photos) for over three years. Lionel worked on the famous Alaskan Highway and then transferred to war zones in the Aleutians where he worked as flight maintenance mechanic and participated in several battles mainly Attu, Kiska and Dutch Harbor. None of this information was known to us. We had last heard that he was in Alaska and assumed he remained there because all his mail came through Spokane, Washington. Any and all information dealing with where and what he was doing was omitted by him completely in all his letters or cut out with razor blades by censors in Seattle. He finally returned home on furlough in late 1944 only to be sent to the Pacific in time to serve in the invasions of Iwo Jima and Okinawa. We thought he had gone back to Alaska. In all this combat he was never seriously wounded, but he never talked about any phase of the war and we stopped asking early when we saw him jump into some bushes when a tire on a passing car blew up. Before he died he finally talked about his ordeal with my son as we drank a bit of scotch whiskey on Christmas Eve a few years back.

For some time we wondered why his letters were so evasive about the questions we asked. We finally figured it out. My family had very limited educations. They were all literate but self-taught. My sister-in-law was native of Tampa and spoke English from birth because her mother was from Philadelphia. She was very intelligent with excellent grades in school so she was a lot more knowledgeable about things "American."

When the attack came that fateful Sunday morning, none of us (not even Anita) had any idea where the hell Pearl Harbor was. I was playing in a concrete sandbox the Housing Authority had built for kids behind some of the apartments at the Ponce de Leon Project in north Ybor City. Several 10 and 11 year-old boys were enjoying an acrobatic exhibition by a well-built, blond, older girl named "Trilby" who was wearing a blue dress and white panties. Nature gets to kids before parents do.

Anita received a letter from my brother every week. Periodically, within the red, white and blue envelope there was a short note for my mom. Exchanging letters with a son at war depended entirely on a 10-12 year-old, skinny, 114-pound kid (up to 118 by war's end)—ME! Mama could not write in English and Lionel, her first-born American son, could not write in Spanish. Is English the unofficial, official language in the United States or what? My mother would dictate to me in Spanish and I would write her message in English. The reverse took place when a letter came to her at which time I translated verbally to Spanish. Mind you, it was household vernacular, but nonetheless a marvelous bit of education I could never have gotten anywhere else. When I went on to high school and college the "foreign" language requirements were a joke. The final exam in advanced Spanish at Tampa University was always a long sheet of verbiage written in Spanish to be translated to English. The rapid fire of my bilingual pen drove the rest of those poor single-tongued, disable wretches insane. I enjoyed the extravagant luxury of loving my country in two languages as war correspondent.

Chapter Seven

Work and Play

I can hardly remember when I didn't have a job of some kind. In my family working was as normal as walking, so as soon as you could, you began earning something to help the cause. That is perhaps a bit of an exaggeration but not by much. I was selling newspapers or shining shoes by my eighth year. Delivering milk, bread; loading trucks, roofer and carpenter helper, banana boat loader, airplane and auto washer, house painter, filling station attendant . . . are only a few of the jobs I've had. When work slowed down in one area, I moved to another. I have the distinction of saying that I was never fired from any job for not being industrious.

Of all my early jobs, the most memorable and exciting and most persistent was being a "hop boy" on a milk truck. Now there's a unique employment that no longer exists. A "hop boy" is as extinct as a brontosaurus rex. I loved it and I was damned good at it, if I say so myself. Two truck drivers almost came to blows over who I would work for. For a poor kid living within the confines of Ybor City and an occasional visit to Palmetto Beach or West Tampa, traveling all over town was like joining the Navy and "seeing the world." Hanging on to the side of a panel truck with both toes sunk into the lip of the running board so I could use both hands to place empty bottles into the slots of milk cases, transfer ice, throw empty cases back and line up the proper amount of quarts of milk for the next delivery—then hop off the truck while it's still moving, dash to the customer's house, place milk (sometimes 4 quarts) pick up empties, run back and jump on a slow moving vehicle—was a great adventure to me. My antics on the running board of that moving Ford panel truck made any circus acrobat pale in comparison. You could have sworn I had an orangutan origin. On top of all that energy-burning joy, I was able to see such exotic Tampa neighborhoods as Hyde Park, Tampa Heights, Davis Islands and rich "tide water" residences along Bayshore Boulevard and Palma Ceia which my driver/milkman, Walter Roberts called "Muskrat Gulch." That's where most

"Hop boy" for Pine Grove Dairy during school years. The painting is a gift from lifelong friend and talented artist, Albert (Skippy) Gonzalez.

of the "pirates" of the Gasparilla Krewe played golf, sailed boats and flew little airplanes. No customers in Ybor, West Tampa or Palmetto Beach, we bought evaporated milk in cans to put in the *café con leche*. Fresh milk came later, another treat made possible by the prosperity that World War II brought.

What I loved most about "hopping" milk was the freedom I felt hanging on to that wagon at high speed (as high as sixty coming out of Davis Islands) traveling through streets and alleys doing my balancing act as Walter negotiated curves. I do believe he sometimes had forgotten that I was hanging out there. A cool breeze (sometimes very cold wind) in my face and a song in my heart, I was in paradise. I had found a way to go someplace else! It was like the feeling I got when I got my first bicycle, first car—freedom, freedom, freedom, it was freedom!

Not all fun and games. I had to pedal a borrowed bicycle at 4:00 a.m. to the processing plant, load the red Pine Grove truck with cases of milk then wait for Roberts to finish his breakfast and read the paper. He lived in the house next to the plant. His family had owned Sunnybrook Dairy which they sold, kept three trucks, four milk routes and named the new enterprise, Pine Grove Dairy. After delivering the route, we returned to the plant where I unloaded all and readied the vehicle for the next day. During the school year, I worked on weekends (Saturday and Sunday) full time. On weekdays Walter would drop me off at school. Regular days were 6 to 8 hours, depending on the size of the route for which I was compensated $1.25. School days I got .75 cents for delivering half the route. I "hopped milk" off and on from age 11 through high school. After graduation, I took both routes as milkman/driver until I joined the Air Force. I delivered a quart of chocolate milk to a girl I was crazy about. She didn't drink it (threw it down the sink drain) she just wanted to see me deliver it to her house in Wellswood. Her mother wanted her to gain weight and went along with the ploy. I married the beautiful Cerelina (Sally) Alfonso and have lived happily ever after in a Wellswood house just a few blocks from my chocolate milk caper.

Walter Roberts was a very funny and wise man in his own countrified way. He laughed loudest of any human I know. Another "cracker" that had a profound influence on my life. We talked a great deal about all things. Although he never converted me, I owe most of my knowledge on the Bible to him. He was a very active Jehovah's Witness.

My other "most favorite" job came so unexpectedly that I thought I was dreaming. Airplanes had always been my first love. One hot June day just out of junior high school for summer, I took the 15th Street bus to Davis Islands. End of the line was Peter O. Knight Airport where I could hang around and look at aircraft to my heart's content. With a little luck I may have gotten the chance to see the Eastern Airlines twin engine, Silver Fleet passenger plane, DC-3. My eyes dazzled, my mouth watered and my heart raced as I saw it land or takeoff. It was a Thaddeus Toad reaction. It was big, it was silver and it was beautiful. I fantasized sitting in the cockpit with my spotless blue uniform—then I would dream . . . and forget who I really was . . . . "This is your pilot, Captain Jack Espinosa. We are making our final approach to Tampa and should be landing in just a few minutes. Please fasten your seatbelts, observe the no smoking sign and remain seated until the aircraft comes to a full stop at the terminal. Thank you for flying Eastern it's been a pleasure to serve you . . . ."

When I got off the bus I wandered over to one of the two hangers on the north side of the field. After getting close looks at several airplanes, I noticed a rather big woman in a man's work shirt, coveralls and a bandana on her head. She was in back of one of the hangers using a small putty knife to scrape paint off an unattached airplane wing. It was so hot you didn't want to breathe. Stood close by for a while watching her work. I finally got enough courage to talk. "You need any help?" She looked up, wiped perspiration from her forehead making sure she got none of that horrid paint remover on her pretty face and said, "I damned sure do son." My isolation mentality could not believe what I had just heard. To me the chances of an Ybor City Spanish kid getting a job at an airport was beyond all possibility. She had no idea what she had just done for me. I would have worked for no pay just to be around airplanes! After recovering from the shock, I was ready to start then and there. "You can start Monday. How much do you want?" Hopping milk I made $8.25 for a seven-day-week, so didn't expect too much. In the stupor of the moment I had forgotten that my parents may not be too willing to let me work around airplanes. I was speechless. Before I could say another word, she blew a curl from her forehead that had slipped out of the bandana and said, "I'll give you $25.00 dollars." THAT'S TWENTY-FIVE DOLLARS—with Saturdays and Sundays off! I knew that the tariff this lady was going to pay for my services would make my folks forget all about the imagined dangers. My excitement was such that there was no way I could have waited for the bus. I took off like a P-40 and galloped all the way from the airport to my home in north Ybor City, a distance of about 6 miles—nonstop.

Teasing my parents a bit, I informed them that I had gotten a job at the airport as a helper/cleanup man. "What? Not around airplanes. Are you crazy, You'll get killed." Papa Salvador gave me his usual, "*come mierda.*" "*Que vuele un aura tinosa*" (let the buzzards fly), he snorted, cigar butt hanging from its usual position on the left side of his mouth.

"But Papa, they're going to pay me twenty-five dollars a week!" A great silence came over all and after a brief five seconds, my mother exclaimed, "Shut up, Salvador, the boy knows what he is doing!"

"Your mother is right," he said. "You are too old for me to be telling you what to do." The twenty-five bucks made me the top earner in the family. Of course, $20 went for the household. I kept the rest for movies and the Matinee Dance at the Centro on Sundays.

Snapshots of biplanes at Fette Aircarft Service, Peter O. Knight Airport, Davis Islands, Tampa.

I took the early bus on Monday to make sure I got there on time. Waiting for Mrs. Fette to open the hanger door one hour after my arrival was not a problem for happy me. I forget Mrs. Fette's first name because I never used it, but I think it was Elizabeth (Betty.) The business was Fette Aircraft Service owned and operated by Mr. (don't know his first name either) and Mrs. Fette. Her husband looked like Ned Sparks, a popular movie comic famous for never smiling. I never saw Mr. Fette smile—never. I washed and cleaned aircraft engines and scrapped paint off of airplanes using that infamous paint remover called Turco. One of the mechanics accidentally sat on some that had spilled on a bench while he was having lunch. After some very serious screaming, he ran to the rest room and stuck his butt in the toilet to put out the furnace. When he came back we noticed that his ass had been erased!

The Fettes owned another hanger in Venice, Florida to which they flew me there to work at different times. Many times I broke the promise I had made to my folks that I would not fly. I could not resist. Imagine my delight to don a flying cap and goggles (like the Red Baron) and sit in the front cockpit of the single engine Fairchild or, better yet, a Stearman bi-plane trainer! Most of the pilots they hired to take airplanes here and there were stunt pilots and they often rehearsed their tricks with me on board just to see if they could make me sick. It was heaven.

I worked at Fette Aircraft Service three summers. I was ready to quit school and move into the hanger. That's when Mrs. Fette put her hand on my shoulder and said, "Jack, that Aircoupe (my favorite airplane) is just like a beautiful woman, it'll take you away from where you need to go and ruin your life. You will never work for me again if you don't go back to school." With all that grease on her pretty face her sincerity came through her pale blue eyes. She loved me like a son. Another person in my life that made a difference. By the time I graduated from high school, the business had moved and my life was heading in another direction. I was too poor to afford any kind of training anyway, but I'll never forget her kindness and concern. I love Mrs. Fette.

Chapter Eight

Movies

During that period of my life I refer to as B.C. (Before Car) there was really only one "official" form of entertainment. It was the movies. All other recreation was self inflicted. There was time for rubber guns made of broomsticks with clothes pins for triggers and a strip of tire tube for ammunition. Model airplanes of balsa wood or "flying" models made of thin wood frames covered with paper were built by those who could. More common were street games like "riqiti" "clee, clee," "lata" and regular ones like touch football and tag. We especially enjoyed playing tag in trees, bleachers, or huge billboards that had lots of iron supports. Idea was to play regular tag swinging from the supports without touching the ground. Cascaden Park bleachers were perfect. We used them as a jungle where we monkeys could swing from rail to rail. My buddy, "YeYo" left the ring finger of his right hand on one of the bolts when the steel ring he was brandishing got hung. What a trip that was as we carried him piggy back to the Gonzalez Clinic, hand wrapped in his blood-stained shirt. We kept his finger in a bottle of alcohol for weeks as exhibit "A"—monument to his stupidity.

A lot of time was spent looking for coins in the sand. Our mock naval battles used the sand of Ybor City (lawns were very rare) as the ocean and pieces of wood as ships. I had a piece of two by four—an aircraft carrier! All this and many other inventions that blossomed in our imagination was what we used to play during the week and on Sundays. But Saturdays—ahhh, Saturday was the big payoff—the movies. Missing one Saturday was slow death by strangulation. The whole week's agenda depended on what we saw on Saturday at the Ritz or Casino movie houses. I became Flash Gordon, Lone Ranger, Spy Smasher, Capt. Marvel, Superman, Zorro—sometimes for weeks on end. I even hummed the music as I donned capes, masks (old towels or rags) flew around with outstretched arms or rode broomsticks (Trigger) depending on which hero was vogue. As we got older movies remained our main source of entertainment with radio a close second. Radio later became my constant companion. Masterful things were done on radio. *Lux Radio Theater* did movies so real that you missed very little by not seeing them. Such great programs as *Hit Parade, Inner Sanctum, FBI in Peace and War* and so many more kept us entertained. Radio's marvelous gift was developing our imagination like classical music does. I'm sorry my kids missed it.

Must have been around five when I went to my first movie though I remember nothing about it. I know it was a western because I've been a cowboy all of my life. Those movies made all American boys cowpokes, even the immigrants. It wasn't long after our birth that we started looking like horseshoes. Nobody rode a horse but all of us walked like we had saddle sores. Only horse I saw in Ybor City during my young life was the nag that pulled the ice cream wagon. I carried a "side arm" pistol made from a piece of broom stick nailed to a wooden handle until my father bought me a pair of silver, cap-firing six guns and holster. I wonder how many times I said, "Draw, you side-winding rattlesnake," to one of my pals. I was the fastest gun on 11th Avenue.

My earliest recollection of movies was going to the Ritz Theater on Seventh Avenue and 15th Street in the heart of Ybor's downtown. As usual, brother Hector took on the responsibility of taking me there every Saturday to see a western, a murder mystery, a serial chapter and a cartoon. My grandmother would pay for my weekly fix. She gave me one nickel for "*la entrada*" (entrance) and another nickel for "*la salida*" (exit.) A ticket to get in and a hot dog and root beer at the *Ritz Corner Sundries* on the way out. No way to measure the colossal impact movies had on my life. Next to public school, movies were most responsible for my "Americanization." This became more apparent during my later adult years and more recently when I see some of those old movies on television. Some of the expressions I thought were my own invention were picked up years ago in movies I had seen in the 30's, 40's and 50's and neatly placed in my sub-conscience for later use. The panic I suffered when I saw King Kong, Dracula, Wolfman, or the Frankenstein monster has turned into comedy. Those space ships I was so impressed with in the Flash Gordon serial that I bragged to my kids about now look like the cardboard toys they were.

Missing one single chapter of a serial was catastrophic. It almost happened once when I contracted one of those little pesky fevers little kids get. Denied as long as I could, Mama somehow knew when I was sick just by looking at me. She would put her hand on my head or (sure fire) put her lips to my forehead. Trapped like a rat. Then came the cures that we now know were worse than the illness. Hoping against hope that the damned fever would vanish before Saturday was torture. Thermometer measured a measly line above normal on Friday night and it appeared I would not see whether Flash would save his beautiful partner from the clutches of Ming the Merciless. No amount of begging, crying, crawling, praying helped. The tyrant of the household would not budge! Anything close to fever warranted an eternal quarantine. Any step outside the confines of your house was considered mortal. Especially true after sundown. You might get *sereno* (something bad that afflicts only Spanish or Cuban people). My chances of going to the Ritz were nil.

God is good. Another angel in my life came to the rescue in the form of my brother Hector who somehow convinced Mama Virginia to acquiesce. I dared not get too excited for fear that my fever would jump up. With two sets of clothes, a cap and wrapped like a pronto pup inside two blankets and a quilt, Saint Hector carried me on his back five blocks to my heaven—the Ritz Theater. My dear brother has been a greater hero to me than the Greek warrior that was his namesake and that trip on his back more heroic than Homer's Odyssey!

When I got a little older and able to go on my own, I followed movies I liked to the various theaters. Movies opened first at the downtown theaters on Franklin Street. The famous Tampa Theater was starting point for all the first class pictures, then they would work their way to Ybor City usually the Ritz. Except for Saturdays the Casino (Centro Espanol) showed movies in Spanish filmed in Mexico or Argentina. Every community had movie houses to include Palma Ceia, Sulphur Springs, Seminole Heights and West Tampa. I took buses or walked as I followed my favorites to the various show places within my range, then I took advantage of the trip by seeing the movie two or three times. I memorized the parts of all the actors and then performed the show for my friends. Two of my favorites were *Up in Arms* starring Danny Kaye and *The Princes and the Pirate* with Bob Hope. I can still remember some of the lines. All this came in very handy later when I went into show business. I did Danny Kaye numbers pantomiming his records until very recent performances at benefits and other shows at Tampa's Performing Arts Center. For immigrant kids, movies were secondary education after public school. Most of those pictures had good triumphant over evil, promoted fair play and justice for all. Hollywood had a big part in molding good, productive citizens and helped pave the bridge between my father's country and mine.

Movies somehow lost their luster when I bought a 1939 Plymouth with my 1950 income tax return. I paid $52.00 for the car I lovingly called my "covered wagon" because the upholstery on the ceiling sagged so terribly that back seat passengers could not see out. A can of brake fluid was constant companion next to me in order to refill the master cylinder under the floor when I lost my brakes. With two glass windows missing, the fresh breezes flowed in and filled the loose upholstery like sails. It was wonderful because it gave me the freedom I had yearned for so many years. At age 18 I resolved that all movies were to be seen exclusively at drive-in theaters where they would be summarily ignored while serving a higher purpose. Who could have known that the internal combustion engine and moving pictures would join forces to bring me to full manhood. Ah, for the good old days!

Book III

Somos Como Somos

El Guajiro, Andres Garcia, vegetable and fruit entrepreneur in truck with no locking doors under pile of merchandise. Credit was available. Debts were kept in small notebook written in pencil and often lost. He got paid anyway. Photo courtesy of Andres' son and dear friend, Esteban (Steve) Garcia.

Chapter One

El Pico

"Cuban Bread" is another one of those misnomers that are used so much that they actually become an accepted part of our Ybor and West Tampa "Spanglish." This came to my realization when I asked for a Cuban sandwich in Havana while there to appear on television show back in the 50's. The waiter thought I was joking and responded smartly, "all the sandwiches here are Cuban just like us." The bread was nothing like what we got from our bakeries back home. The stuff between the slices of bread depended on what you wanted. Ham and cheese, egg, chorizo and a popular mix they called "*media noche*" (midnight.) No Cuban sandwich. The bread made in Ybor City by the Segunda Central, Ferlita bakeries and a few others was uniquely Tampa. "Americans (those who were not us) mistakenly thought that all people who spoke Spanish were Cubans. Logically then, the bread made by Spanish-speaking people was referred to as Cuban bread. Same happened with the sandwich which was another original and was correctly called sandwich "*mixto*" (mix.) There is wide difference among natives as to exactly what went in to the original Cuban sandwich. My first recollections go back to the late 30's when I was sent to Los Helados De Ybor to buy sandwiches *mixtos* for the men who met at my godfather's (Eugenio Fernandez) house on 11th Avenue right next door to mine every night to discuss all matters. His front porch was like a neighborhood coffee house where everybody gathered. The sandwiches I ordered contained pressed ham, roast pork, Swiss cheese, salami, a slice of turkey (yes, turkey) and two thin slices of sour pickle. Bread was either buttered or spread with mustard as ordered. Lettuce and tomato was a later addition and only upon request. All ingredients were very sparse. It was the combination that gave its unique taste. The fact that economic conditions were a bit tough had a lot to do with the amount of meat and cheese. They were a great deal shorter than the current ones too. Mayonnaise was in the making as far as we were concerned back in the early 40's. My grandfather thought that mayonnaise was the French national anthem.

If I had named this work *Tampa Bread Crumbs* nobody would have known what the hell I was talking about. So, as my dear friend Tom McEwen would say, "nuff said." Cuban bread it is and I can't live without it. It's our vitamin "C."

Loaves are about 30 inches long and no one can handle it without leaving crumbs. And . . . you must consume the loaf on the same day it is baked or it can be used as a lethal weapon on day two. No killer has ever used Cuban bread as murder weapon because the evidence would cover the crime scene. Notice waiters at Spanish restaurants with napkin hanging on their forearm to clear tables for the next customer. Many used a knife from the dinner table to clear the crumbs. Each loaf has two points (picos) which my wife prefers. I put her on when I ask her, "which *pico* do you want me to save, the front or the back?" Like life, it has a beginning and an end. Which end is the start and which is the end depends on the point of view of the consumer. When the word *pico* is applied to the cigar business, it's the number of cigars a worker could take free of charge at the end of the day. Numbers varied from two to ten. My mother always supplied papa with three or four *picos* a day.

I pondered for some time on how I was going to end this work of love I have called *Cuban Bread Crumbs*. The angel that writes jokes for me appeared in a dream and suggested that my last chapter should be a depot for the few short stories still whirling about in my deranged mind. You might say that these last ones are the crumbs from the end *pico* of that delicious loaf that has been my life, or the last few hand made cigars by mama's skilled hands. These tidbits are intended to give you a few more peeks into the lives of that first generation of children from immigrants to Ybor and West Tampa and *porque somos como somos* (why we are as we are.)

Chapter Two

La Medicina

After getting settled in the New World and a job secured, the biggest problem was health care. Those coming from Spain or its Cuban colony (The Pearl of the Antilles) left countries where medical care was available through mutual benefit societies. Members paid a fee to receive complete coverage including medicine. In Tampa the same famous societies were established providing total care from doctor home visitation, through nursing home (more of a "sanatorium" since most kept elderly at home.) The four big ones, Centro Asturiano, Centro Espanol, Circulo Cubano, and L'Unione Italiana had big dance halls, theaters, gaming rooms complete with bars and coffee shops. Some had gymnasiums, handball courts; sponsored baseball and softball teams, and boxing matches. These societies operated out of beautiful buildings much to the pride of members who paid a very reasonable weekly fee. Membership was open to anyone who cared to join. There were also two clinics, El Buen Publico and the Trelles clinic providing only medical care but similar to the others, they included doctor home visits or by appointment, medicine, surgery and hospital care. It was better than nothing and at times pretty good, depending on the seriousness of the affliction. Besides, our illnesses were very simple and at times as unique as our personalities.

For a while, everybody that checked out died of tuberculosis (no matter what it may have been), heart failure or from a *santinbeque* (probably a stroke.) There were other illnesses suffered exclusively by Cubans or Spaniards like a *sirimba*, I still don't know what the hell that is, but I know it was bad. We also were the only humans to suffer from *un aire* (an air.) Ray Toledo was pulled out of a basketball game holding his ribs in excruciating pain. Coach Bill Stewart asked him what was the matter. "Coach," he replied, "I got an air." "A what?" Coach then assumed it was gas. "No coach," said Gil Tomas from the bench, "it's not, *un pedo atrabezado* (a trapped fart) it's an *aire* (air.) Ray got an air and he's got a pain in his *vaso* (glass, like a drinking glass.) I believe "the glass" is a spleen. Stewart never understood what it was all about. None of us die of a *santinbeque*, or a *sirimba* any more, nor do we suffer from "airs" since we've become Americans.

For most of us, as I recall, we had either a cold or an indigestion. The cures for these ailments were established and immovable. For *catarro* (cold) it was a dose of castor oil usually mixed with orange juice so you would hate OJ forever. An *indigestion* was taken care of by half a glass of Epsom salt mixed with water. Either of the two "cures" mandated your sitting on a toilet seat or a potty (*el tabor*) regularly for the next three days. In case of fever you were really in for it. The treatment was repeated as much as necessary and if persistent—bad news. It meant that the ultimate clean up treatment would be administered. The dreaded *LAVADO!!!!* Your own mother turned into a member of the Inquisition torture brigade to force feed a mixture of castile soap and water through your rectum using a long hose attached to a tank and a horrid black *piton* (spout) lined with Vaseline. After a long chase and battle, the deed was done, but not quite over. Now the victim was required to hold within the walls of his intestines what seemed like a gallon of liquid as long as possible. To let go too soon meant another attack. You held on, and on, and on until the sadist gave the long awaited signal. The bombastic explosion that followed was as welcome as an admission to paradise or a one year pass to the Ritz Theater. Prayers followed that the fever would subside and that you were not afflicted with any semblance of a sore throat because Madame de Sade would wrap cotton around a stick that looked like a telephone pole, soak it in iodine, (the skull on the label said it all) and then shove it down your throat to the esophagus while you gagged for air. To accompany all this torture, no solid food was to be consumed, only broth (*caldo*) with no noodles! After seven days, you looked like a corpse. Our loved ones gave credence to the adage that says, "the cure is worse than the illness."

There is a standard joke that I used for years that applies here: My grandmother suffered from a very bad cold and an indigestion with fever. Treatment was the big three since the first line of defense against these ailments was to "clean you out." When the doctor came by a week later to check on her condition, he found a bouquet of flowers on the front door. He asked my father how the old lady was getting along. In typical Ybor vernacular, Papa told him that she *canto El Manicero* (sang the Peanut Vender.) The last words of that song *"me voy, me voy . . ."* ('I'm going, I'm going) the vendor's voice dims as he leaves. It is used to mean that you are going, going, gone—dead. Upon hearing of grandma's death, the doctor gave his condolences and asked, "when is the funeral?" Papa replied, "as soon as she gets through shitting we're going to bury her."

"*Jaibita calientica*" (hot deviled crab), a familiar sound in old Ybor as Francisco (Oscar) Miranda hawked his delicious offering. Looking on is a fellow street vendor, Andres Garcia (*El Guajiro*) and friend Manuel Valdez. Photo taken on 7th Avenue (*La Septima*), courtesy of Esteban Garcia.

Chapter Three

Some Unforgettables

Unforgettable characters came in bunches like bananas in Ybor City, too many to mention in several volumes to text. There were also unusual sounds that were exclusively "ours." Street vendors were plentiful and each became a part of the sights and sounds of our community. Each hawked his wares in very unique manner. There was no confusion about what product was being offered. Jorge Miranda, the deviled crab man, donned all in white walked and later (when business boomed) bicycled his way through the streets. His call was a beauty. No doubt what was for sale when two blocks away you heard, "*ja-a-a-aivita, ja-aivita, jaivita clientica,* hot debo!" It was a sound never heard by the ears of man, something perhaps close to a tenor fog horn with laryngitis. To the outsider, there was no way of knowing what the hell it was about in spite of the fact that Miranda's call was bi-lingual. *Jaibita* is Spanish for "little crab." *Calientica* is "caressingly hot," almost like saying, "hotsy." Note the ita at the end of the word *jaiba* (crab) and the *ica* at the end of *caliente* (hot). These endings give Spanish words a little more flavor. Then (in case there were English-speaking people about) he would end the call with the English word "devil" except that he pronounced it "debo." Get it?

Piruli Man walked the streets holding a six-foot pole at the base. Stuck into tiny holes on the pole were long, cone-shaped, multi-colored crystal candy lollypops. A tall, magnificent, rainbow-colored tree loaded with delicious pirulis (pee-ROO-lee) was the offering. It was a beautiful sight, like something out of the Land of Oz. A marvelous treat and you could have one of the fruit from the magic tree for a penny. I don't know who the Piruli Man was. He never said much. His coming was heralded uniquely as he played the musical scale up and down on what looked like a large harmonica. He would then yell out in Spanish, "*con dinero, o sin dinero,*" (with or without money.) In lieu of currency, he accepted coupons from evaporated milk cans that could be traded for prizes.

A horse-drawn carriage came by during those long summer days when I spent most of the afternoon playing on our large front porch. It was a welcome sight. The sway-back nag that pulled it brought ice cream and sherbet if you had a nickel. Two sugar cones each crowned with one large scoop of your favorite topping. Abuelita Carmen saw to it that I had the medium of exchange when early on she slipped me the nickel. I never deviated from my favorite delight, *albaricoque* (apricot) sherbet. It was so good that I hesitated consumption. I fought the urge to devour with all my strength so that the moment would last as long as possible. No matter how hard I tried to extend the pleasure, Ybor's unbearable summer heat worked against me. Who said happiness can't be bought? My grand kids came close to that kind of happiness when I bought them a car! I can still feel the glorious anticipation when I heard the slow "clomp, clomp" of that old mare coming down the red-brick street and familiar "ching, ching" of the little bell on the wooden covered wagon with rubber tires. Hard to believe that a human being could be so happy with so little.

An old Sicilian vendor grew vegetables on a small plot of land just east of Ybor City's imaginary border. He was stone deaf. I never knew his name other than *El Versero* (Collard Greens Salesman). Old and deaf, he still pushed a very large two-wheeled cart full of collard greens up and down brick streets all day long. In long, low-pitched monotone he would hawk his vends in Spanish, "*versa, versa, a la buena versa*" (collards, collards got good collards) repeating the call over and over and over. Customers would yell loudly from their porches (most houses had a porch) hoping to stop him so they could buy. To no avail—he couldn't hear them. So, on he marched in rhythm with his call, "*versa, versa, a la buena versa.*" Only way you could negotiate a purchase was to dash out in front of the wagon and wave. It became another unforgettable Ybor City-ism still in use today. It is used when someone is spoken to and does not respond, continuing his way uninterrupted as though he never heard you. "I told Facundo to stop drinking and womanizing, but he "*a la buena versa.*"

Fishmonger, appropriately nicknamed, "Pargo" (Snapper) brought seafood right up to the front of our houses. His call was heard four blocks away, "*peeeescadoooo, feeeeeesh.*" Pargo would filet and scale fish right in front of you with a very sharp, long knife. Fish were on large chunks of ice in long boxes in back of a truck. Kids would jump on a step at the back of the vehicle to suck on the pieces of ice that Pargo would chip off to make us happy. It was never as plentiful as was the case with the ice man who brought blocks of ice and placed them right in your ice box. We mistakenly called him el *nievero* because we confused ice (*hielo*) with the Spanish word for snow (*nieve*.) The ice man carried huge chunks of ice covered with sackcloth and used an ice pick to mark and then chip off the exact size block to properly fit the customer's ice box. If you wanted to buy ice by the pound, he could do that, too. With the precision of a surgeon, he'd simply chip off a chunk that weighed pretty much the amount you wanted. My dearest friend, Joe Chao, was a carrier on an ice truck. Small and skinny as a rail. He would put heavy blocks of ice on his minuscule shoulder, protected only by his shirt and a piece of sackcloth, and deliver it right into the ice box. Things got a bit tough when he had to climb stairs to apartments or rooms in multi-storied buildings. In most cases delivery was made on certain days depending on the time of year. "Ice man," was the call as they entered the house on the due date to make sure there was nothing too personal going on or occupants not properly clothed. Icemen had very interesting stories to tell.

Silent man of the group was the taffy man. Never said a word, at least I never heard a single sound come out of the little stout man in the white suit and hat. One of the great mysteries of my life is how in the hell this guy managed to be in so many places. For a little fat guy, he sure got around. I could have sworn that he was in more than one place at the same time. Ybor, Downtown Tampa, in front of theaters, dances, fairs, funerals—he popped up like a leprechaun. Instead of a pot of gold for those who caught him as Irish folklore has it, he offered delicious, little white rocks of hard taffy that he chipped off a block with a tiny hammer and then place in little bags. The load of candy was carried on a small platform connected to his waist and held up by a strap around his neck freeing his hands to chop, fill bags, hand candy out, collect money and give change. Unbelievable! Ten cents a bag was a bit pricy, but at times irresistible.

Chapter Four

Los Carros

To all this color add the sound of the streetcars, out most important and at one time the only mode of transportation. If there is any visual that can be used as Tampa's signature, it's the streetcar. It is to my generation what cable cars are to San Francisco. I still miss them terribly no matter how impractical. By design, the lines connected all the cigar factories in Ybor City, West Tampa and Palmetto Beach providing access to these for cigar workers. There was one long line that went straight down the Bayshore Boulevard making it possible for our African-American brethren (mostly maids and yard men) to get to Tampa's "tidewater residents." Theirs was a very difficult trek from the area northeast of Ybor to their destination. My family used it to go see our sick at the Central Espanol Hospital on the Bayshore. It took a trip downtown via the 12th Street streetcar and then a transfer to the big one that rocked down the Bayshore Boulevard all the way to Ballast Point. Fare was five cents each way. For the kids it was a great thing, but for workers unlucky to live far from their workplace it meant getting up very early, enduring long hot or cold trips before starting on the job. The way back home was just as bad or worse especially for many women who still had cooking, dishwashing and children to tend. Don't know how they did it.

Streetcars were slow by today's standards, but it was exciting to hear them rumbling down the track with a power boom reaching up to a small wheel that rolled on a wire above the street. The wire provided the electricity to power the car and it stretched the full length of the route just like the track. When it got to the end of the line, the conductor (dressed like Ferdie Pacheco) would reverse the seats, connect the throttle to the opposite end of the car, take down and secure the boom to what now became the front and then loosen the boom from the back and connect it to the wire. Since both ends of the car were the same (to include lights) there was no need to turn around. You simply reversed seats, power connection and throttle. Like a loaf of Cuban bread, it had two *picos*. Together with the noise made by steel wheels rolling on steel tracks, occasional sparks from the boom touching the power lines, and a very peculiar odor which I believe was caused by the oil used to lubricate various parts, streetcars were not as romantic as they appear today to nostalgic people who never had to ride one. The lubricant smelled like castor oil, a familiar, unpleasant fragrance that made some people sick. At one time or another every kid I know threw up in a streetcar. Why do I love and miss them so much? Because they are an integral part of my very young life—what we old farts refer to as the good old days. Some of us are beginning to understand that what was so good about the good old days was that we were young!

As you may surmise after my meager attempt to draw a word picture of what a streetcar looked like and how it operated, those quaint yellow transporters were very vulnerable. Like a docile behemoth sea cow, it took very little to disable them. Once the boom was disconnected from its power source (a live electrical wire above), it was dead in the water. More often than I care to admit, we would spend hours filling paper bags with sand mixed with a few Ybor City sandspurs and then wait behind a concrete fence at the St. Marcus Methodist Church on 16th Street and 12th Avenue for the streetcar to stop and pick up commuters. If there were non, we'd send *"Chancleta"* (Malcolm Echevarria) out there to pose as a passenger while those assigned the task would unhook the boom. Usually done at dusk, all lights went out and the streetcar sat helpless. Before passengers could close the windows, at least two volleys of sandbags were hurled at the helpless trolley. After the bombardment, the attackers would flee the scene of the crime as the poor conductor, covered with sand and spurs walked around to reconnect the beast and bring it back to life. How thoughtless, how terrible, how irresponsible, how DELIGHTFUL!

In Palmetto Beach, a peninsula that juts into McKay Bay just south of Ybor that we referred to us as our "appendix" (a useless connection to the intestine), a designation highly resented by those who lived there, there was a "gang" that copied our antics. The streetcar that went in their direction rolled south on 22nd Street from 7th Avenue, connecting three cigar factories with workers from outside the area. Palmetto streetcar dead-ended at DeSoto Park. We referred to the kids there as "fiddler crabs" because there were so many of them around the mangroves that hugged the peninsula. Blue crabs were also abundant and sold by the sack full off little shacks jutting out on wooden piers.

Joe Chao was a native of Palmetto. The "Fiddler Crab" was almost my clone. We are so much alike. We came from similar parents, we were both the first generation children of immigrants, both forced into early adulthood and both of fiery independence and wacko sense of humor.

He and a band of ruffian "crabs" were harassing the streetcar line in their neighborhood to the extent that Tampa Electric Company executives contacted the city councilman from the district to see if something could be done because the police could not find the culprits. Rumor was that Chao was the lead crab and difficult as it was they finally got to him. Not an easy search because, like a crab, he could crawl forward and backward and live in a hole. The councilman and the principal of Phillip Shore Elementary School spoke to "King Crab" and after much deliberation and denials an accommodation was reached (unprecedented in the history of Ybor City). Joe Chao, 10-year-old citizen terrorist from Palmetto Beach, forced his terms upon the power structure of Tampa. He was to be allowed to drive the streetcar from 7th Avenue south on 22nd Street to the end of the line with full control, pick up passengers and . . . free to ring the bell (controlled by a pedal) at will. In return he was to call off the sandbag attacks and other harassing antics on Tampa Electric streetcars forever. The agreement was consummated . . . . HOW CIVILIZED! . . . much to the delight of the "Crab" who for many years bragged about bringing the power structure down to its knees, especially after a few libations around our camp fires. We were born at the best of times. Wonder what would have happened to the "Fiddler" today?

Benino (known as *Beneno*, venom) Gonzalez stands in front of his famous feed store ready to take on the world.

Chapter Five

B. Gonzalez & Perez

During my early teen years I spent some of my spare time at a feed store on the corner of 15th Street and 24th Avenue in north Ybor City. Owner and manager of the establishment was the beloved and most unforgettable Benino Gonzalez. Benino looked like he had just got off the ship that brought him from Spain many years back. He also had a nickname, but no one dared to call him by that designation. We called him *Beneno*, which is a misspelled reference to *veneno* (venom or poison) due to the ferocious temper tantrums that made him famous throughout the community. The kids thought it was hilarious entertainment and spent much time figuring out ways to anger him without getting hurt.

His son and my close friend, Jaime, is built like a fire hydrant, stocky and powerful, handsome of face with lots of long black hair. He worked helping his father at the feed store lifting heavy bags and loading trucks since he was old enough. Both were very strong and could punch like the kick of a Missouri mule with both hands. Jaime and the legendary, Tony Marchese, whose father owned a saw mill, were just the ticket when a fight broke out so long as they were on your side. Both were especially effective in a free-for-all, what we called a *"sal pa fuera"* (a "get out.") I saw Jaime hit a man that was giving me a hard time at the Dream Bar on Nebraska Avenue. The guy was very tall and well built. I was getting ready to do what I could with my 118 pound (but wiry) frame. Jaime, shorter than all of us, moved in like a stroke of lightning and ended the situation with one robust shot to the side of the guy's head. He hit him a second punch on top of his head as he went down. When he came to, he did a lot of funny things trying to get away from Jaime—tore the knob off the front door doing all he could to head west at full speed. He did more harm to his body trying to get out of that bar than the two punches Jaime had inflicted. We never saw him again.

Benino, his father, was the block from whence had come the chip. Only difference was that Benino (Beneno) was born in Asturias, Spain, spoke very little English and had an even shorter fuse than the kid—dynamite! His business was very tough work and we kids were not very welcome around the store. But because his tirades were such a show, his own son was the main instigator in the planning and execution of some terrible tricks. When angered (it didn't take much) Benino had a very novel way of showing his displeasure. Red-faced he would bend both of his short legs at the knees (like he was sitting) put both hands palms up down between his legs, then take short jumps as he pumped both hands forward and up as if throwing his testicles at you. As he did this he'd be cussing in Spanish at those responsible for his fit. The hops were in rhythm with his dialogue. It was one of the most spectacular sights ever beheld by man.

Of all the many contrivances we inflicted on poor Benino, the one most popular was the time we placed a phone call from the drug store across from the feed store and ordered bags of feed to be delivered. The caller was his own son disguising his voice. He gave price, wrote down name, address and then loaded the several hundred pounds of cattle, poultry and rabbit feed onto the truck. Off he went with name and address of the "customer" in hand. After going around a few times, he parks in front of his house (half block from the feed store) and realizes that the address we gave him was his own! All of us, including his own flesh and blood, were hiding in bushes, behind trees and concrete block fences on 15th Street and 24th Avenue to see his spectacular reaction to our shameless shenanigans. I can still see the look on his face when he finally realized how he had been taken. It was vintage Benino. He turned off the ignition, jumped out of the truck while it was still in motion and before all who were around or driving by he did his hop, stroking his crotch area as he cursed. "*Me cago en la madre de todos los hijos de la gran puta que por aqui estan escondidos.*" "I shit on the mothers of all the sons of grand whores hiding around here."

Jaime later became very successful as owner and operator of an auto body shop and wrecker service (Acme Garage) still located just a few blocks from the old feed store location. Some years ago as I drove by I got off to chat with my old friend. He was carrying his beautiful baby daughter. The little girl was apple of her proud father's eye. After we spoke for a short time, I hugged the baby ever gently. As he went to put her in the truck, she accidentally struck her head on the door. Baby screamed and cried, papa caressed, put water on the bump and lovingly rocked her till the crying subsided. Still whimpering, he went to put her into the truck's cab a second time. Again she hits her head on the top of the door. As the baby bawled Jaime hands me his precious cargo and then attempts to comfort her by sternly looking at the door and saying, "Don't worry, mamita, this door will not hurt you again," as he beat the truck door with his fist making several huge dents. Little Cynthia stopped crying. Unforgettable!

Chapter Six

Nombretes

A psychiatrist would have died of malnutrition in our town. Not that we didn't have a goodly share of nuts, it's just that nobody cared and they were somehow worked into our lives. Besides, everybody was a bit coo-coo so it all appeared natural. There was a mass inferiority complex which I believe was the direst result of just being "foreign" which may explain why we were so sensitive when signs appeared that read, "NO LATINS OR DOGS ALLOWED ON THE BEACH." Now that's enough to give Superman a complex. Two ways to show inferiority, you either bow down and cower or you stand up and bite back. Like all other humans, some of us chose defiance (sometimes to the extreme) and others kept silent to stay out of trouble. In any case, by the time we grew up the ignorance on both sides was conquered by knowledge as is always the case. Like all other minorities, discrimination brought us closer and much to the credit of the best system in the world, my kids never felt the pain of that injustice. My generation has pretty much overcome the stigma that prejudice leaves, but here and then the chip on our shoulder raises its ugly head. Among us, however, it would have been difficult to find anyone too sensitive for too long.

If you happen to have the misfortune of being lame your nickname would be *El Cojo* (pronounced *Coho*—Lame.) My father-in-law's brother has a real name, but I still don't know it and neither do most of his life-long friends. *Cojo* is what he answers to with no sign of discomfort. When he calls on the phone he says, "hello Jack, this is *Cojo* calling from New York." There are many still called *Flaco* (Skinny) in spite of the fact that they have gotten fat over the years. Among the more familiar are included: fat guys (*Gordo*) long-nosed (*Narizon*) *Bemba de Chivo* (Goat Lips) *Rompe Navo* (Turnip Buster) *Cara de Fango* (Mud Face) *Cabezon* (Big Head) *Boca de Cherna* (Grouper Mouth) *Diente Frio* (Cold Tooth or Bucktooth) *Boca Buzon* (Mailbox Mouth) *Bombillo* (Light Bulb) *Culito de Pollo* (Little Chicken Ass) *Culo Cagado* (Shit

Ass) *Mangera* (Water Hose—wonder why they called him that) . . . and many, many more. Notice that I listed the more classy ones toward the end. Beauty of this is that those nicknamed actually accepted their given designation with little or no resistance and responded to those appellations when called. *Culo Cagado* (Shit Ass) was a highly respected member of his community who owned and operated a very successful filling station and auto repair service in West Tampa. I must add here that his nickname is one of those terms that do not translate well to English. It sounds a lot more acceptable in West Tampa Spanish—it's almost caressing. My mother-in-law was called *Boca Buzon* (Mailbox Mouth) but I never addressed her in that manner. Mine for years was "P-40" because I had a face like a Flying Tiger. I also answered to *Mosquito de La Draga* (McKay Bay Banana Dock Mosquito.) If you stuttered you were *El Gago*, cross-eyed, *Visco* and everybody, I mean everybody was at one time or another called a *come mierda*! English translation of that nomenclature is rather repulsive. Those who do not speak Spanish may find this beyond the bounds of common decency but believe me, it's not at all bad in Spanish and you may use it liberally when appropriate. The term has been so popular over the years that the real meaning has lost its filth and expressed rather nonchalantly. It is really used to mean "buffoon" or "foolish" "dummy" "unintelligent" but the direct translation I dare to say is "shit-eater!" You can be a little stupid, "un *pocquito come mierda*" or a big fool, "*tremendo come mierda*." I have often used it when exaggerating a person's ignorance. "He studied to be a *come mierda* and graduated with honors."

Chapter Seven

Dragon Follies

My three years at Jefferson High School were the best years of my life. It was the final stage of my metamorphosis from a Spanish-speaking, frightened, confused and angry son of immigrants to a young American ready to take on the world. The delicious admixture of Spanish, Sicilian/Italian, Cuban, Jewish and all those others that we called Anglo-Saxon or Americans (as if we weren't) created a superb atmosphere for learning. Jefferson High, so aptly named after the father of our democracy, had about eight or nine hundred kids, a very small student body for a high school. It's what made us proverbial underdogs. Every school we competed against in all sports were bigger and better equipped. Although not apparent to us at the time, it was a perfect fit for the immigrant kids. We had never had very much and having to cut out a piece of the action in a world that was unfamiliar and at times unfriendly, we were comfortable and proud to be at a disadvantage and still kick ass. The atmosphere was electric. We "Latins" and our new found "Crackers" joined as one to prove to the universe that we were all Dragons.

If anyone questions the value of sports, I tell them the story of how sports, like war, brought us together. Our coaches, Dick Spoto, Sam Alfieri, Bill Stewart and others marshaled that angry energy and directed it to the playing field and out of the streets. We owe them and all of our teachers a debt of gratitude impossible to ever pay. They understood us and rolled with most (not all) of our shenanigans for which we were famous. Our tricks were mostly played on each other. We never disrespected our teachers, we loved them. When I hurt my knee and had to quit the track team my senior year, it was a hard blow. Yet, it was a great and most meaningful turn in my life. Loving all sports and now unable to participate, I turned to writing about it. This brought me in touch with a most influential individual and the major reason that I am writing this story.

She was my journalism teacher, Ann Lang Ayala. A thin, intense, intelligent dynamo with an uncanny insight into what makes people tick. Ayala knew my leanings, told me how to best do it and then got out of my way. She was the reason *The Jeffersonian*, our weekly, four-page school paper took All-American honors on a steady basis. As sports editor, I wrote a column called *Days Later*, in which I told it like I thought it was. When we got screwed out of the state baseball tournament in spite of having the best record, I smelled a rat. With the help of a few coaches and a little research, I uncovered the scheme and exposed some of the officials responsible. When I wrote in my column that it was "the rottenest, filthiest scheme ever dragged out of the gutter," (perhaps a bit childish and over dramatic) I was called in by the principal who scolded us both for attacking important officials of the Big Ten Conference. When he mentioned throwing me out of school, she was ready to go with me. Her retort was clear and concise. My analogy may have been a bit pointed, but the facts were pure truth, she said, "besides, how can we preach freedom of the press if we ourselves don't defend it." How's that for an educator. She stood up to the principal on a matter of principle. Here's another example of an American "Cracker" (her maiden name was Lang) defending justice on behalf of a son of immigrants. I will never forget her.

Tampa Tribune, our life-long daily newspaper until the welcome addition of the *St. Petersburg Times*, had sent their crack photographer, Sandy Gandy, to take pictures of me after I had a rather auspicious start on the track team. The Tribune's famous sports artist and cartoonist was going to honor my efforts with a sketch. I was justifiably proud even though my parents never knew anything about it. They only read the Spanish weeklies (*La Gaceta and Traduccion Prensa.*) Their world was now separating in earnest from mine. I had once gotten home very tired with three gold medals earned in a track meet. My father was cutting some little pipes in the back yard with a tiny hacksaw. When I approached, he asked me where I had been. He had forgotten that I was going to compete in a "*juegos Olympicos,*" which is how I described it so he could understand me. I put three gold, a silver and two bronze medals on the cut tree trunk he was using as a work table and told him of my exploits. His unlit cigar moved magically to the other side of this mouth and then asked, "*cuanto te pagaron por esto?*" (how much did you get paid for that?") "Nothing," I replied. Cigar moved up and down in rhythm with his lips as he said, "*eso es una mierda.*" ("That is a piece of shit.") I laughed and laughed. Papa never understood what was funny. May seem harsh treatment or even child abuse to this generation, but to mine it was downright hysterical. I've told the story many times. It is indicative of the distance between my "Curro"

Spanish father and my All American grandchildren. Can you imagine what my placid wife would have done to me if I had asked one of my kids how much they got paid for getting a homerun—and then saying, "big shit?" I would have been summarily "funeralized."

Sandy drove up to the old Jefferson High building in his new miniature Crosley automobile right on time. Members of the track team (all ten of us) were sitting barefooted by the south entrance. It wasn't very smart to put on track shoes and then walk to Plymouth Park city playground several blocks away. Spikes on those shoes were made of steel, very long and thin like big needles. The "track" was a measured 440 yard oval on park ground mostly sand from the rut cut through the grass by runners. We lovingly referred to it as "The Great Dragon Sahara." No gym, no track, no body-building facility or program and definitely no stadium. No matter. We were fighting Jefferson Dragons, the toughest, meanest sons of bitches in the galaxy. We didn't need all that fancy crap to kick ass. Our athletes were as good as any in the state. We had something nobody else had, a gigantic chip on our shoulders, a bad junkyard underdog attitude, and two men named Richard Casarcs and Indy Cuesta. Casares is unquestionably one of the best athletes ever to come out of Tampa and the State of Florida. Superstar in all sports, he was particularly outstanding in football and basketball. He was "all everything" every year but in his senior he was All City, All County, All State and *All America*! As a professional, he is considered one of the great running backs for the Chicago Bears. Indy could have been a star pro too if he had pursued it. He was Rick's blocking back in high school and one of the reasons for his spectacular success.

Camera in hand, Sandy Gandy set up tripod and got me positioned for the takes. The rest of my team, including Casares went about doing what we had planned the day before. They picked up Sandy's Crosley, carried it into the building, placed it squarely in the center of the auditorium stage and closed the curtain. I joined them at the "Sahara" after the photo session. His car gone, Sandy ran to the pay phone on the corner of a drug store close to the school, called the police and took a cab back to the Tribune.

Juniors had charge of the assembly the next day. I was the master of ceremonies for a short variety show. The band brought me on with a spectacular fanfare. I got to the microphone, welcomed the captured audience of over 700 Dragons, did a couple of gags and then with the voice of a circus ringmaster blared out, "and now fellow Dragons, it is my esteemed pleasure to present to you the star of our show, SANDY GANDY'S CROSLEY!" The joint stood up and roared as the curtain opened. What a moment!

Before we were all put in the slammer, we announced that we had bought Sandy a gold watch in payment for any suffering we may have caused. Half the student body had been in on the scheme and donated money the week before to buy the watch. Sandy took it like a man and cheerfully accepted the gift. He never pressed any charges though he often questioned our sanity. I suppose that he accepted that we "somos como somos."

Chapter Eight

Louie

Louie Lopez was one of those "best friends" that we had when we were kids. Lucky us that we had so many, most people outside our time zone have just one. Ybor, West Tampa, and Palmetto Beach kids born in the 30's and 40's know what it is to have hundreds of "best friends." It is one of my great treasures. Louie, Tony Munoz, Charlie Gustafson (El Craca) Tony Reale and myself made for a very special quintet during my years at old Jefferson High School. Our relationship went back to elementary school, but two summers picking tobacco in Connecticut really cemented our camaraderie. We shared the same dormitory room and some of the terrible things we did during our tenure up there are legendary. The affection we had for each other was for real. It was one for all and all for one under any and all circumstances, but being as we are (porque somos como somos) some of the irreverent atrocities that we inflicted on each other remain some of the funniest memories that we enjoy.

Our main and exclusive interests were food and women, and not always in that order. The lust for opposite sex was like a great bubonic plague that hung over us. Abstinence was our curse. Don't think that our generation didn't want to, it was just that the rigid customs of Spanish, Italian/Sicilian and Cuban immigrants denied us the opportunity. They watched us like hawks and without cars it was virtually impossible. Of course there were some cases in which "will" provided "way," but it was rare. There was that story about a woman being impregnated through a chain link fence, but it has never been verified. For most of us, sex was prohibited by the girls whose parents had painted a very dismal picture of what their future held if they succumbed in the HEAT of a passionate moment. The guys didn't give a damned about any dismal future, so in our society, it was the woman who kept us decent. A little kiss was difficult when you can see the white undershirt of her father through the porch window. That kind of restriction provided chaperones for everything. It was either her kid brother or her mother that tagged along and even when alone you had to take her to the movies in a bus or streetcar. Her old man had the trip timed to perfection. If curfew was not met, it required long explanations. What can you get away with while walking down a sidewalk and all the neighbors looking at you from their front porches!?

There was a link in the armor. It was called "dancing." I figured that if you stand in front of a woman and rub up against her, she'll slap the hell out of you, but, if you put music to it, you can get away with it even as parents watch. The whole gang learned to dance. Ah, the dance, which I define as a "dressed rehearsal." Dances were packed. I spent all week in school and working as a "hop boy" delivering milk off a truck yearning for the Sunday Matinee Dance at the Centro Espanol where I could glue my skinny body onto some pretty girl. My reputation got around and I remember mothers sitting on the sidelines at the dances airing themselves with little Spanish fans warning their daughters, "*No bailes con Jack, se pega mucho.*" ("Don't dance with Jack, he pastes himself too much.") Everybody danced the "slow pieces" because these provided best opportunity. When Don Francisco's Band played "Star Dust" it was a mad rush to get that one gal you had been eyeing. It was volcanic. At the end of the dance the guys looked like an army of hunchbacks getting back to their tables. Pants of those not wearing jockstraps looked like army tents! How embarrassing! At the intermission, most of the guys had it timed to take off during the last selection to avoid having to pay for a coke and Cuban sandwich or whatever the young lady you had been dancing with may desire, especially if she brought her mother along. At the end of those glorious moments, the band played, "Goodnight Sweetheart." I still feel the melancholia I felt when it was over. Last dance had to be with that very special one. It's one of the reasons we refer to those times as, "the good ole' days."

Because society denied us what nature had ordained, the desire of anything "sexy" was highly exaggerated. Opportunity to experience the tiniest bit of anything sexual was often taken at great cost. Old Jefferson High School had an auditorium that doubled as a basketball court. The games were played on the stage. Fans sat in regular auditorium seats as though watching a stage show. Our "ghetto" school was next to last in getting any allocation for such frills as basketball courts, track and field and even football practice facilities. Our Afro-American brethren were (as it was then) always in last place. The auditorium floor (backstage) was very large, well varnished and shinny. When we found out that the girl's physical education dressing room and showers were located directly under the center of the floor, plans were immediately begun to drill a hole through which we could at least enjoy some view of what we craved for and lived for.

Here's the plan: Four stand guard on each end of this huge court floor (backstage); make sure the curtain is closed; one peeping Tom gets on all fours in the middle of this huge floor and peek through the hole for three minutes. All agreed to the sinister scheme. The sentinels stood watch as Charlie (our token cracker) drilled the hole with a long hand drill he had "borrowed" from the shop while Mr. Rowlahand (teacher) slept. He had not slept too well since the time we had nailed his wooden leg to a desk one afternoon while he slumbered. Drilling seemed to take an eternity because work had to stop when Mrs. Campbell (nicknamed F.B.I.) came by patrolling the area. She was better than Jacobo's hound finding class skippers, trespassers and profane wharf rats like us.

Charlie had done the best he could but the hole was really not wide enough. A peeping Tom had to be very lucky to see any living form unless it was directly below the opening. Fat chance. We made sure the girls were out playing volleyball while we drilled so no debris would fall through the opening and thwart the project. Diabolically clever, we had thought of everything. When we checked to see if something could be envisioned—we saw absolutely nothing. We figured that lights were off in the showers making it impossible to see. Hope hung on. Truth was (although we didn't know it) that the drill was not long enough and the light at the end of the tunnel was coming through the sub floor.

D-Day and Louie had won the toss after some squabbling as to who deserved to go first. Four guards stood at their stations at each corner of the basketball court. Little Louie scampers to the middle of the court, gets on all fours and puts his face flush against the floor. Left eye closed, he places right eye on the hole and s-t-r-a-i-n-s trying to push his eyeball through it to the other side. His butt up in the air, head on the floor and eye fluidly sinking into a small hole, Louie is like a short ostrich in its most vulnerable position.

At this unlucky moment, Tony spots Mrs. Campbell down the hall marching toward the backstage entrance. He whistles our Bob White (bird) signal warning all to abort. All of us save little Louie, too intent on his dastardly mission, heard the alarm and abandoned our posts, leaving Louie to fend for himself. Now why would we do a thing like that? If he had been drowning, like George Benitez was when he accidentally slipped off the Hillsborough River dam, we would have jumped in to save him as we had for George (I almost drowned pulling him out.) This was different. It was not a life threatening (apparently) or serious injury matter. We looked at this as an opportunity to see Louie sweat and more importantly, to see how the little bastard was going to handle the matter. It was beautiful. Here's Louie glued to a floor with absolutely no possibility of being unseen and less chance of escape. How magnificent was our comrade's vulnerability—in total disregard of the world around him—lost in the vile hope of even an infinitesimal moment of feminine ambrosia. The cowardly four that had betrayed him cowered behind the curtain in splendid, delightful expectation. Campbell tiptoed toward Louie's prone body like a Siamese cat, then stood there like the Rock of Gibraltar looking straight down at his now twisted body straining laboriously to catch one measly glimpse. A bit of compassion befell me. Suppose Mrs. Campbell chokes him? The blood would be on my hands. Too late, so be it. After what seemed forever, he finally lifted his head up to ease the pain in his neck. I was at a perfect angle to see the look on his face when he noticed Campbell's right toe, now tapping lightly on the floor. His eyes seemed much, much larger than I had remembered. If he had been a British soldier at Bunker Hill, Louie would have been the first casualty. The white of his eyes illuminated the darkness of the entire court. Slower than an arthritic sloth he rose from the floor. Not a word was said as the F.B.I. stood there with one eye closed peering at a sorrowful-looking Louie with the open one, her mouth perked to one side and arms folded. I could almost hear Louie thinking as he finally stood up. He looked like Droopy, the sad-sack dog from the old cartoons. Now—here it comes. Louis Lopez, citizen soldier of the Republic of Ybor City takes a deep breath, exhales forcefully and says, "IT'S AROUND HERE SOMEPLACE."

Taking a few more steps, he makes believe he has lost something in the middle of this vast, clear, shiny floor. Just before the inevitable deluge he adds, "It's my lunch money, I dropped it around here." Last-ditch effort to appease, to find some pity on Campbell's grim face had failed. With the speed of a Bengal Tiger, she went for the jugular. Last we saw was poor Louie being dragged out with F.B.I still clutching his throat. "Why are we so unscrupulous with our own flesh and blood" we asked ourselves as we roared with laughter? Because Louie would have done exactly the same to us . . . and because . . . *somos como somos.*

Chapter Nine

Double Pleasure

Bilinguals double their pleasure. Sounds like good adage to put on a bumper sticker. It's true. Those fortunate enough to speak two or more languages may understand what a great advantage it is to communicate (and therefore think) in more than one idiom. It gives existence an additional color, a delicious sauce denied to those unfortunate souls anchored down to only one mode. Translations, however expertly, never really do it. There are words that do not translate accurately and since words are humanity's most common form of thought transmission, translations from one language to another are attempts to express not only items common to all but intangibles such as thoughts, customs and feelings. "*Te quiero mucho*" translates literally to English, "I care much for you." For those who speak both languages, the English version of the same tender feeling sounds a bit cold. To make it hotter, Spanish may give the word "much" a substantial boost by adding five more letters to "*mucho*." By placing "*isimo*" at the end you get "*muchisimo*" WOW! English does not boost the word "much," it requires another word like the adverb "very" to warm it up a bit. Not that English can't be passionate. Just read "Romeo and Juliet." If some of those scenes don't warm the cockles of your heart nothing will. (There's nothing worse than cold cockles!) English is a superbly rich language because it is a product of the merger over centuries of German (Anglo-Saxon), French (Norman) and substantial Latin word derivatives. But it is basically a Germanic language. Spanish is less of a mixture, based mostly on Latin (Romantic) with an Arabic touch. Without some long dissertation on the subject, for which I am unqualified to address, if you are lucky enough to have even a modest command of the two languages, your life will be much more interesting for you. If you can handle three (English, Spanish and Sicilian/Italian) as some natives of Ybor or West Tampa can, you are really among the blessed of this planet.

Jose Rosas, my step-grandfather, in his 80s, hoping that a sufficient amount of knowledge of the U.S. Constitution has penetrated his large, round, hard head.

There is a down side. If you spoke Spanish or Sicilian for the first five years of your existence, you will never be quite free of the accent your first language hung on you. I don't consider an accent to be a handicap. On the contrary, a pronounced one is often seen as charming depending on the language and education level of the individual. Look what it did for Fernando Lamas (*ju arrr marrrboloos*) and Ricardo Montalban (*Corinthian leather.*)

My dear friend, the late Cesar Gonzmart, would enhance his Spanish accent and trot it out whenever pretty, English-speaking ladies would show up at the Columbia Restaurant in Ybor City. He usually led with, "Senorita ju arrr veeri charrrming," before making his violin weep for them as he stood on his tippy toes. Cesar, an accomplished musician who, together with his wonderful wife, Adela, (also a first-class musician) were owners and operators of the world famous Columbia Restaurant. I often joke about a very talented singer who was a featured act at the restaurant for years. Antonia Curbelo has a beautiful tenor voice and a very charming Spanish accent that worked well for him. When he sang the popular American song, "Feelings," he pronounced it "Fill-ins." "Fill-ins, nowsing more dan fill-ins, trying to forget ju fill-ins of love . . ." as the song goes. Every dentist convention dinner in the U.S. was booked at the Columbia to hear Curbelo sing "Fill-ins" was one of my standard jokes, especially when I worked the Siboney Room at the Columbia as stand up comic and pantomimist for shows, club dates or speaking engagements.

Most people with those attractive accents are embarrassed about it. That's nonsense. They don't realize how beautiful and how acceptable it is. Fact is most people appreciate a foreigner's attempt to communicate in their language. I performed in Havana on Cuban television and night clubs during the late 50's. My act was in English, but because I could speak Spanish, I was able to get along mostly doing the pantomime part of my routine which featured miming recordings by American artists such as Spike Jones, Stan Freberg and other musical comedy stars. It was a big hit in Cuba because all those strange sounds (such as hiccups, sneezes, snorts, etc.) appeared to be coming out of my mouth. I had opera numbers in which speed changes were taped to give it the "chipmunk" sound.

I was very fortunate to have had the opportunity to work in Cuba and it all happened by accident. Strictly an American act working night clubs in the U.S. for some years, I got involved with a group of entertainers appearing in Tampa at the Royal, Casino and Cuban Club Theaters. The artists were mostly sons and daughters of Ybor and West Tampa residents. The promoter was a popular Spanish radio personality, Ruben Fabelo and he had made connections with a large daily newspaper in Havana (*Diario de Las Americas*) to send a troupe of entertainers from Tampa as a goodwill gesture, being that so many of the acts were doing Spanish and Cuban music and dance. When we were auditioned, those chosen made a guest appearance on their top TV show that very evening. I was lucky enough to be asked to return. The program was top rated variety show, *Casino De La Alegria*, on which I appeared regularly during the mid to late 50's. I was there when Batista fell from power and Fidel Castro took Cuba. I had the pleasure of appearing on the same bill with some great American entertainers. Among them was one of my old time favorites, the fabulous Nat King Cole. He was very concerned about his American accent when he recorded a long-playing album entitled, "*Saludos a Mis Amigos.*" It was a collection of some of the most beautiful music produced by Spanish-speaking songwriters. He was worried that his Spanish was terrible and that this would hinder acceptance by the Latin American community. I told him not to change one word. He was never going to overcome his accent anyway and the songs sounded even better with his charming accent blending so magnificently with his uniquely melodious voice. The great Nat King Cole sang their songs in their language! An army of diplomats could not have had a more positive impact on relations between our county and theirs. It sold millions in all of Latin America. So much for accents.

The real disadvantage for bilinguals is vocabulary. There are tons of words in each language. To become efficient in more than one is very difficult. Being born of parents who spoke only Spanish became a great barrier during those first years in school. Kids, however, learn at lightning speed and by the end of the second grade I was teaching my elders how to speak "Americano." Those who are so afraid of losing English in their country should understand that it takes only one generation to "Americanize" our fellow immigrants. English is the unofficial, official language and will remain so. Public school takes care of each generation. I and my family are living examples of that. When I graduated from the University of Tampa I was recipient of an award for maintaining the highest point grade average in my major subject (History.) After giving a brief acceptance speech, my father hugged me and through proud tears said, "*Hijo, hablas un ingles magnifico.*" (Son, you speak a magnificent English.) He felt more "American" because he had an English-speaking American as a son. It was that way with the rest of us folk from that generation of immigrants.

Besides, we always knew that we had a piece of the action when we learned that the Spanish had opened this hemisphere to Europeans over 100 years before the English got here. By the way, the Mongolians were already here waiting for the Spaniards. "Our Mongolian pilgrim fathers," doesn't sound right, does it? I am reminded that our American forefathers, who were mostly sons and daughters of English, Scotch/Irish and German immigrants were so angry at the Anglo mother county after American independence that a bill was introduced in Congress to make German the official language! It lost by a scant few votes. The First Amendment of the U.S. Constitution guarantees freedom of speech in any language. In the case of recent (1960's) Cuban influx, it took no time at all for them to catch on. We now have former Cubans and other Spanish-speaking people who speak enough English (with accents) to be senators, representatives, governors, and high ranking government officials at all levels. In California we even have a German-born naturalized citizen of the United States who has a monstrous, yet delightful, accent. He does, however, govern in English. By the way, don't get nervous about the huge recent entrance of Asians, they are doing very well here with their broken English and their kids are even better (winning all the spelling bees.)

In Ybor and West Tampa, many of our elders had to depend on their children to handle things outside our environs. Not too much mail came to my address but when it did it was in English so either myself or my much older brothers handled the situation. When a uniformed mailman stepped onto that big wooden porch, put something into a flat black mailbox and blew a whistle, it was a matter of great importance at 1611 11th Avenue. It was THE GOVERNMENT calling. For people that had nothing but bad experiences with government in their native countries, it was very serious. My folks hadn't yet learned that in the United States, government is servant to the people, not the other way around. After my brothers married and left, I became a very important member of the clan. At age ten I was the only "man" in the family who could handle all things "English." Imagine what that did for my psyche!

There is a funny side to all this. During that inevitable transition from foreign to American there are hilarious situations. Ybor City being an admixture of cultures, produced some of the most side-splitting misuses of the king's English. I can afford to poke fun at these indignities because I have at times been as guilty as my brethren. As we learned from each other, very interesting things happened to the English our poor instructors were trying to teach us.

As long as we remained within our "colony" there was little problem with language. Spanish was of course dominant because the two largest immigrant groups (Spanish and Cuban) spoke Castilian. Sicilians being a minority within the Latin community, picked up Spanish fairly well, at least enough to be understood. We often joked that English was a foreign language in

Ybor City. Back in the 30's and 40's that was not much of an exaggeration. In fact, there were stores on Seventh Avenue (*La Septima*) that prominently exhibited signs that read, "ENGLISH SPOKEN HERE" to lure American customers. But if we went downtown, it was a different story. It was a rare thing during my early years to come across a bi-lingual outside West Tampa or Ybor. We got along anyway. A clerk at the Kress store on Franklin Street tried very hard to satisfy my mother's request for a colander. I stood by, a bit embarrassed at mama's attempts to communicate in pantomime. Nine year olds are not mature enough to see much humor in watching what my little brain erroneously viewed as my mother make an ass of herself in public. She could care less. She was going to make this poor little freckled face girl understand one way or another. After providing sounds and visuals of water going through a pot with holes in it, and attracting half the customers in the store to watch this unusual spectacle, mama took a pause. Her face lit up (as if the angels had provided her with a celestial key to the riddle) and said, "Me want one macaroni stop, water go!" "Oh, of course," said the clerk as she reached under a pile of kitchen utensils behind the wall and brought out a silver colander. The crowd, now close to twenty people, applauded. My mother took a bow while I was walking away trying to be somebody else. For many years my family and many friends referred to a strainer (colander) by that handle. "Hey, where the macaroni stop?" or "Get the macaroni stop out of the drawer for me," terminology that makes dinner guests at my house scratch their heads. It opens the door to very funny conversation. Then there was the time my father, asking for ground beef, pointed to a piece of meat and told the English-speaking butcher, "Please, put these for revolution in the machine." It worked.

My grandfather, Jose Rosas, never attended school. He was barely literate in his native tongue (self-taught), so you can imagine how tough it was for him to learn a new language especially in his late seventies—impossible! He had a terrible time with pronunciation because English, unlike Spanish, is not phonetic. You don't pronounce it like you spell it. Where do we get the sound "thawt" out of "thought?" We don't pronounce the "g" or the "h" in "night" or the "k" in "knight." The dilemma became acute indeed when it was required for immigrants to answer questions in English on the Constitution of the United Sates posed by a judge in a courtroom full of applicants in downtown Tampa. The building (post office) made of solid rock and multi-storied was to immigrants a frightening show of power as was the bearded, imposing, long "Americano" in black robe who never smiled and spoke in a thunderous voice. Poor Jose, he tried so hard. It was pathetically funny. *La Gaceta* and another Spanish language weekly newspaper of the time *Traduccion Prensa* printed a list of questions and answers in English on the Constitution likely to be asked. Imagine me, an eight or nine year old child, reading questions to my grandfather on that great document. "Who makes the laws?" I would read from the newspaper page glued to a piece of cardboard. "The leche-leche," he replied. "Leche, leche" is "milk, milk" in Spanish. Close enough. "Who executes the laws?" "El presidente." Who interprets the law?" "The sucreem court." . . . . And so on.

Armed with his knowledge of our great contract, Jose Rosas gallantly attacks the windmill. He had told me that every Spaniard has a *Quijote* in his soul. And so, with my father at his side, (like Sancho Panza) Jose rises from his seat when his name was called. He was wearing his best clothes, a black suit a bit too large for him loaned by his friend Manuel, who rented a room at our house and seldom paid. A vest that appeared to have one thousand buttons, white shirt, tie wide enough to cover most of his chest, a pair of high-top black work shoes that looked like the ones worn by Dr. Frankenstein's creation, a gold chain hanging from his belt down to the crotch and then up to a watch attached to it and nestled in a small pocket, a black derby adorning his large, bald head all composed the rest of his morbid array. On the way to the "execution," as he passed a large painting of our first president hanging high on the wall, he tips his derby ever slightly and says, "good evening" to George Washington in the vile hope of scoring a few brownie points with the judge. He had not learned to say "good morning" yet.

First question: "Mr. Jose Rosas, when were you born?"

First answer: "Harrruuup (clearing throat) July 4th, 1776!

The judge did not blink. My father sighed and looked up to the ceiling. Immigrants awaiting their turn laughed nervously at Jose's answer. A calamitous start. After several other questions, the judge returned to the first and asked him again, "When did you say you were born?" This time the old man understood the question and gave him the date of his birth. It was the only question he answered and only the second he had even responded. Twenty more minutes of questions followed for which Jose had no answer or even a hint of what the hell the judge was talking about. "Regretfully," the judge empathized, "your father has not advanced to an acceptable level yet." He advised my father to help him study a little more and return next year for another try. My father grabbed the old man by the arm and led him out. As he passed by Washington's painting again he bowed ever slightly and said, "good evening, Mr. Way-chin-ton." When we got to the hall, Abuelo Jose, my first pupil, asked meekly, *"No lo hice bien?"* "I didn't do well?" Before I could respond, Papa replied in typical Asturian manner, "No . . . animal." We all laughed when my father told Jose that the judge must have thought that he was Jesus Christ—born twice. Back to the drawing board.

His third attempt had been moved up when the rules allowed less time between tries. This time, much to our shock, the same judge came off the bench shook Jose's hand, patted him on his large, hard, bald head, handed him his citizenship papers and told him, "With two grandsons fighting for this country, you are just as American as I am." Jose Rosas had no idea what the judge said, but he grabbed the papers and hurriedly walked out of the federal building after the usual greeting to his old pal, "Good evening, Mista Presidente."

All my immigrant family, except my grandmother who was too sick, became American citizens . . . and they did it with the help of a 9,10, or 11 year old kid that learned enough English by the third grade to do it. It was one hell of a start for me. Most people in this country have never read the Constitution, much less understand it. Still, those of us who learned the language of our parents from birth were handicapped for most of our lives. For those who went into fields that were not demanding constant use of English, it was even tougher. Vocabulary expands throughout the years, but only for those who continue the learning process. A person that works in business that has little contact with the English-speaking public and then goes home to his Spanish or Italian-speaking family, doesn't get the opportunity to improve on his English. Sound grammar and proper pronunciation is really not needed to be understood if you worked in a cigar factory, painted houses or worked in construction. I still have problems because in spite of my years in show business as comic and master of ceremonies, teacher, government administrator, speech and program writer, English is so difficult that even individuals far better educated than I (or is it 'me') are not at all embarrassed to ask, "how do you spell that?" That first generation born in America is burdened with a vocabulary-lean English in many cases. Be it far from me to be critical of our misuse of the language of my forbearer's chosen country, especially being a twig from the same limb and root. Furthermore, the assassination of the king's English is not the sole purview of so called Latinos. Many Anglo-Saxon, Irish, Welch and Scotch natives of the British Isles are equally guilty of what Professor Higgins (*My Fair Lady*) called, "the cold blooded murder of the English tongue."

To me the funniest demolition of the Anglo-Saxon lingo is the malaprop. Malapropism is the ludicrous misuse of words that resemble in sound but have different meanings. It is very common among those trying to communicate in a foreign language. Example being when Emilio Lopez, one of my neighbors long ago, was chewing on something while sitting on his front porch swing. When I asked him what he was eating he replied, "a *synonym* bun, you want some?" He meant *cinnamon* bun. My uncle Eufemio put it all together, he called it a "son-of-a-gun." Get it?

Through the years my dearest friends (more like close brothers) Frank and Jerry Alfonso, Joe Chao, and our token "cracker," Dennis Ross, helped me collect malaprops uttered by our families and friends. These four and myself are partners in a hunting camp in the Ocala National Forest near the Oklawaha River. In typical Ybor City vernacular, we named the camp *Blue Bayuo*. Note the malaprop for *Bayou*. *Bayuo* is Spanish slang for a dive, what we used to call a juke-joint or a drinking establishment of ill-repute. No other handle could have fit more appropriately. We are really more armed campers than hunters. The group has been partners in the "Shangri-La" enterprise for over 40 years. Not too many families hang in that long. All of us worked as teachers, government administrators and businessmen. Not a week went by that we did not meet for lunch, a drink or talk on the phone. We've been in touch for over 40 years. For a long time we saw each other at least twice a week. Our time together, even during the worst of time (and there were many) was soothing when things were bad and hilarious always. We've spent decades making fun of each other, somebody or something else!

My favorite exchanges were when we compared the latest malaprops. After offerings of the ones actually heard were presented and time allowed for roaring laugher, we would pick the malapropism of the week. I remember that one of the winners became the malapropism of the year. Three of us had gone to a funeral and as we approached the front entrance of Our Lady of Perpetual Help catholic church, the daughter-in-law of the deceased nervously met us at the door and said, "They got him in the *rectum.*" *Rectory* is what she meant. The three of us hauled ass in different directions to keep from breaking up a very sad affair with insolent laughter.

Instead of listing a long train of my favorites, I decided to here include a letter that my dearest friend (luckily, I have many) Joe Chao and I composed and sent via U.S. mail to some of our friends. If the postal inspectors had realized what was contained therein, we may have been charged with using the U.S. mail for hilarious fraud. It's more than we deserve—much too funny for mortals. I have italicized each malaprop and "Spanglish" expression for those who care to speak like some of us.

Dear Joe,

I was thinking about you as I returned from *Sans Pete* Beach where Sally and I had a delicious *brefus*. Traffic on the *Franklin Howard* was like always, a real *bottle up*.

As you know, I spent some time in the *Bohamas* on *backachon*. My daughter's husband flew us there in his *Piper Club* airplane. They had attended a Republican Party *Carcass* in Miami and used the opportunity to take us across. They turned Republican when he made all that money. Now they think they are real *hay puloy*, you know, like their *fetus* don't stink. While in Miami, we ate almost daily at my favorite *dilly* on the beach. My son-in-law doesn't like *dilly* food. He thinks he's in the *higher-up-archy*, too good to eat in such places. The jackass doesn't realize that when it comes to food, I'm a *common sewer*. Thought of you when I went to see an old movie at the beach. One of our favorites about the vampires starring *Bela La Rosa*. Remember him?

Wife and I stayed in North beach. Nick let us use his *condom*. The place was first class, real *push* with *scrubs* planted in the window *sillys*. He had been building that place in *phrases* following an old *floormat* his brother Gus gave him. You know about Gus. He got in trouble when he worked for the bank downtown. I believe he was getting *kickoffs*. His attorney told him that he can go back to Tampa because the *statue of libertation* has passed and they can no longer *persecute* him. In case you don't understand, that's when a long time has passed since he took the *kickoffs*, not to be confused with the famous statue on *Static Island* in New York. Gus is staying in Miami. He's rich and become a very *impotent* person, even has a *sectary* that *screams* his *phome* calls. He just traded his Ford *Marqueeze* for a new *Buuke*. One good thing he did, he put a lot of the money he stole in *escargot* so his daughter can make use of it when she gets older.

I tell you buddy, some things in life are hard to *phantom*. Our friend Nelson is so stupid. He went hunting for *peasants* and shot into a whole bunch of *cobblers* instead. What an idiot! He's never going to change. Remember when they caught him *evesdripping* in Mrs. Brown's class? Funny! I don't know how the ass got out of the 6th grade, he could never *dilute* any information. I was trying to help him but I didn't want to wind up as his *escape goat*. Mrs. Brown always had a good *sortment* of material even though she was a new teacher, more or less a *green hornet*. Poor lady, I understand that she had a kid suffering from *tuber-culosis* and had to live in a *sterile free* room. Back then medicine was not too advanced, they didn't even have any *angel plastic* surgery no matter how much money you had or how *impotent* you were. I believe people were healthier then because there was less *humility* in the air. People were more polite too. Today everybody talks bad about others, always casting *asparagus* at each other's families.

Speaking of families, Carmela has been taking care of my mother—what a wife I have. As you know mama had serious eye trouble. She was seeing eye flashes through her *rectum*. It was so bad that her driver's license was *provoked*. Dr. Guggino, a famous *emptymologist*, told us that she had a detached *rectum* that can only be fixed by using a *lazy beam*. We are thankful about one thing, her cancer is in *recession*. She still has a hard head. Sick as she is she still got sick after eating two helpings of beef *stroking off* at a Hungarian restaurant downtown. My grandson got stomach trouble too from eating so damned much. We had to take him to a *pipiatric* physician, but because of his age he was referred to an *external* medicine specialist. As it turned out, it was just a severe case of *gastoronomy*.

I take care of my family and I keep my religion. When I die and get *funeralized*, I'll have no *regets*. Can't say the same for my son Antonio. The way he cusses borders on *blastfamy*. I told him to *cease and assist* using bad language. Look what happened to Pete Rose for cussing and gambling. He was *bandaged* from baseball for life. Now it's his turn *under the barrel*. With all he had going for him, he should have used a little more *enginerity*. He should stay away from horse tracks and spend more time listening to *sympathy* orchestras.

Better close now, looks like a storm is coming and I don't have any batteries in my *fresh light*. The old lady is finally going to wash the dishes before they get *toctic* in the sink (ha ha.) Going to watch the History Channel as you suggested. Tonight they are showing World War Two films featuring air battles in the Pacific where we shot down all those *como-wazees* sent to their death by Emperor *Hirotito*, that bastard. General *Macaco* really kicked their ass when he returned to the Philippines. Tuesday it will be the Invasion of Normandy under the leadership of our other great leader, General

Sopaenagua. They are also showing a special on the elections where they will explain the *electrical system* and how presidents are really chosen. I've never understood that. Can't wait for Friday my favorite program about animals. They show actual attacks by lions on zebra and *wildbeasts* in the *Serendipidy Plain.* I hope you saw the special on the great leader from India, *Mohon Mas Grande.* He was one heck of a man.

Oh! Almost forgot. Thanks for the help you gave us in getting Elvira's *segurity* check with your *concoction* with Representative *San Givings* Office (not to be confused with the American holiday when we eat the turkey, *Sangivings).* You were right, it was just a *commuter* problem and she not only received her check, she got it *radioactive* from the time they stopped paying. You deserve all the *escalades* for fixing the problem so quickly. Now the old lady can afford to eat more *fong-do* at the Swedish restaurant (ha ha.) Don't worry about me, I'm an old *geyser* and can take anything. I'm tough like my father. It runs in the family. I guess you can say that it is *genital.* I came to that *concussion* a long time ago not just at the *sperm* of the moment.

Hang in there. Your old pal,
Jack

P.S. Got your Christmas card together with the rest of my *correspondences.*

Chapter Ten

Fin, Fine, Finish

There are thousands of stories about the unique experiences of my generation. The folklore of my people may not be as old or mysterious as the trolls of Scandinavia or the leprechauns of my Irish great-grandmother, Ana Fowler, but in due time it will have its place.

Three major groups of immigrants settled in Tampa in the same areas. This was quite different from alien settlements in other larger cities such as New York where Irish, Jewish, Italians and a myriad other newcomers created specific "towns:" Little Italy, Chinatown, Germantown, Spanish Harlem, etc. In Tampa there were no Italian, Spanish or Cuban sections. Ybor City was named after a Cuban cigar manufacturer. Factories were built in Ybor, West Tampa and Palmetto Beach. Cigar workers through sheer necessity moved close to their work places or rode streetcars conveniently tracking every factory. Businesses catering to those immigrants followed, many owned by people of the same national origin. Most of the grocery stores were owned by Sicilians or Spaniards, but Cuban cuisine (black beans and plantains) were available anywhere and every Jewish clothing store on 7th Avenue featured *guayaberas*. All dances had Spanish and American music. At the Centro Asturiano Cuban rumbas and Spanish paso dobles were played by a Cuban band on the first floor while the "kids" could jitterbug or slow dance (sex rehearse) to crooning ballads on the top floor. At the Italian Club dances there would be added a blazing tarantella or a waltz where an elderly couple flowed from one end of the floor to the other. I went to a Polish dance in Windsor, Ct. when I traveled north to pick tobacco one summer and every single dance was a polka! "Our" dances reflected the uniqueness of what I've called often called "the devil crab" element—the "yellow rice and mangos" mixture that is "us." Those who didn't know us conveniently put us in a "Latin" category in spite of our differences. Lately, the new category for all Caribbean, Central and South Americans is "Hispanic." That's like calling all who speak English Anglo

Saxon. By design or circumstance, my generation of immigrants had to face one another in our neighborhoods and schools. What a heavenly stroke of luck, it's what gave us a uniqueness like none anywhere. When we inevitably mixed with our "American" brethren, the metamorphosis was completed. It is this legacy that we leave to our new American grandchildren.

From our cuisine, "Tampan" language, together with a few weird superstitions like the Ybor City curse, *fu fu el gato*, which I use rather effectively at Buccaneer football games against opposing field goal kickers, to the Sicilian eye, *mal d'occhio*, to our strange cures for illnesses unknown, outrageous nicknames and loving insults (*come mierda*), our incredible sense of humor . . . no one can say we're not different. Looking back at my long trek, I am ashamed to say that during my very early years, before I knew better, I was embarrassed by the awkward behavior of my kin. It didn't take me long to realize how precious their "differences" are and how much those qualities mean to me. It is what gives us "roaches" and "devil crabs" the sauce that makes us interesting and friendly. Among the many virtues I bear with me resulting from my experiences in life are the invaluable friendships I've made. Some people have one or several "best" friends, I am truly blessed with virtually thousands of all nationalities, races and cultures from wherever I've been. Propensity to make friends easily is one of those attributes I owe to my "hometown" security. I have always known where I belonged and where I came from. I had a home plate I could depend on at all times. Our tough times in overcoming discrimination because of our differences also contributed to our sense of character. The pain of being considered inferior is forever with those who suffer from that most unjust form of ignorance, but it does have its reward. It has given me and those like me a great capacity for tolerance, appreciation and even affection for those "different" than us. This we proudly pass on to the next generation of "roaches" so that America may remain the greatest land of opportunity ever known to man.

Hillsborough County, Florida, especially Tampa and my "cracker" love affair, Plant City, are the only places where I can live. I've been all around the United States and many foreign countries, but after a few days away my long nose, like the needle on a compass, slowly points back to 7th Avenue and 15th Street in old Ybor City where I was born under a camphor tree. When the time comes to check out, or as we say in "Tampan" to "sing the Peanut Vendor" (*cantar el Manicero*) I am going to do it in my town.

Printed in the United States
142109LV00008B/106/A